Able to Garden

Able to Garden

A Practical Guide for Disabled and Elderly Gardeners

Edited by Peter Please

Illustrations by Val George

Photos (except where stated) by Ken Day

B. T. Batsford Ltd, London

First published 1990
© Horticultural Therapy 1990

ISBN 0734 6137 3

Typeset by Tradespools Ltd, Frome, Somerset
and printed and bound in Great Britain
by Bath Press, Bath
for the publishers B. T. Batsford Ltd
4 Fitzhardinge Street, London W1H 0AH

CONTENTS

- ACKNOWLEDGEMENTS -

This book is a result of ten years of work by the Society for Horticultural Therapy, advising people who are elderly or disabled on their gardening problems.

The authors are:

Alan Bell
Ed Davies
Rosalyn Dodd
Carole Green
Jane Lesser
Peter Please
Tim Spurgeon
Ruth Tessler
Malcolm Weare

Special thanks also to:

David Hollinrake, Research Gardener,
  Mary Marlborough Lodge
Juliet Vernay
Vincent Robins
RT Herbs, Kilmersdon
Donna Lippiatt

Although a keen gardener from an early age, I have to admit that my serious interest in the subject was awakened while engaged in caring for the disabled and elderly, and had it not been for the encouragement given me indirectly by my clients, my life today could have been very different indeed.

My main responsibilities were for the elderly, physically handicapped and blind, and it never ceased to amaze me what lengths and feats of inventiveness they would resort to in order to indulge their hobby. Many of the persons I visited lived in elderly or handicapped persons' accommodation which often seemed to have unnecessarily large gardens, and yet I seldom heard complaints to this effect. Indeed, in a lot of cases it appeared to provide just the challenge they were looking for, and it was not unusual to encounter rivalry between neighbours – especially when it came to the largest vegetables or most flamboyant dahlias.

In the course of a day's visiting, I would encounter lawns like freshly Hoovered carpets, immaculate rows of vegetables, houseplants so bursting with health that they threatened to engulf their owners, brilliant bedding displays, and chocolate-box cottage gardens which made my own efforts of planning and cultivation – even with youth and physical fitness on my side – seem pathetic.

That was twenty years ago. It seems incredible that my colleagues responsible for occupational therapy were not briefed to offer gardening as a subject in those days! It was left very much to the individual's imagination as to how they tackled the garden with their various disabilities. Tools for disabled people were thin on the ground then, but I encountered many brilliant home-made improvisations with which my gardening-minded clients achieved their aims.

This was my first experience of the therapeutic value of horticulture. It was obvious that persons who derived deep satisfaction from gardening would go to any lengths to keep going. Their enthusiasm was infectious, and it was not long before their pleasure in being close to the soil was passed on to me. My increasing fascination with gardening was to provide a useful bond between me and my clients. Chatting easily about roses, onions or strawberries soon broke, down any barrier which might have been there.

I knew very little about gardening when I began caring for the elderly and handicapped. Before I left, I had gathered enough information on the subject, mostly from my visits to these brave and wonderful people with a lifetime of experience behind them, to contemplate a new career in horticulture. I had entered their homes for the purpose of giving them what assistance I could through my position, and they had collectively given me infinitely more. Today, many of my current 'topical tips' are based on hints given to me during this time, and the progeny of seeds, cuttings and plants pressed on me then are still in my garden today. My technique for taking hydrangea cuttings is the same now as it was when

Mrs G. showed me how. She was well into her eighties and had multiple disabilities. She walked with two sticks, one of which she exchanged for a hoe or a long-handled weed fork while she was gardening. It is a pity that organizations like Horticultural Therapy did not exist in those days to enrich the quality of life of many people like her.

Those who do not understand the subject are often under the mistaken impression that gardening for disabled people and the disabled person's garden are somehow set apart from the way able-bodied people tackle the subject, and yet all that is required to turn the physically fit gardener's technique into one suitable for the handicapped is the appropriate modification. It occurred to me, as I read through the pages that follow, that this book could be useful to all of us;

however agile or dextrous we may be, there are always ideas we could adopt to make gardening easier.

In recent years there has been an increasing awareness of the needs of the disabled gardener, and this has led to the development of some special tools and other appliances. Continuing development should add to the ways in which the gardener with special needs can further explore his love of growing plants. Books such as this and regular interchange of ideas should keep us gardening through difficulties which would have seemed insurmountable a few years ago. For people like me, for whom life without gardening would be unthinkable, what a blessing this is.

Daphne Ledward

Getting started

ONE

Planning for pleasure

Planning your garden for ease and enjoyment doesn't mean calling in a landscape designer. It's largely a matter of common sense – a little thought eliminates a lot of problems. Before you read our 'dos and don'ts' why not see how many you can list yourself with the help of the picture? Then consult the checklist.

Think about design...

A Make sure you can get to the greenhouse and shed from the path and that both are near the house. Can you get in? This greenhouse has a sliding door and the wide double doors to the shed have handles which are easy to reach from a sitting position. Wheelchair users will also need space to turn round outside the door.

B Espalier or cordon-trained fruit trees grown to a height of 1.5 metres (4 ft. 6 in.) can be reached from a wheelchair for pruning and harvesting. Did you know that soft fruit such as gooseberries can be grown as standards so you don't have to bend down to them?

C This prickly hedge is difficult and painful to trim.

D The path is too narrow and uneven and will become slippery in wet weather.

E Tall fruit trees aren't only difficult to reach – they can be dangerous too.

F Narrow borders are easy to cultivate.

G Weeds love large areas of open soil and most of this bed is too wide to reach from the path.

H Tools of the right weight, height and design can make a job much easier!

I A raised edge around the pond wouldn't only be convenient to sit on – it would also make the garden a lot safer.

J Lawns are hard work to mow and the edges are difficult to keep tidy. Have you got the best tools for the job? What about replacing the lawn with paving and ground cover plants?

K These steps are a barrier to a wheelchair and too steep for a gardener with poor balance – they can pose problems for able-bodied people too.

L The cold frame is too low for easy work and its glass top is dangerous.

M Stakes and canes in a flower or vegetable garden can injure a gardener who falls or bends down suddenly. Put a flowerpot or some padding on the top of each cane.

N A raised cold frame with claritex, polycarbonate or perspex instead of glass is accessible and safe.

O Coloured and textured paving cuts out glare and is easy to walk on, even in the wet. For visually handicapped gardeners, different textures provide reference points.

P The steps are replaced by a ramp 1 metre. (c. 3 ft.) wide with gradient no more than 1:15.

Q This happy gardener has got everything right! Instead of hedges, raised beds divide the garden; his plants are within easy reach, either when sitting down or with long-handled tools from a standing position. The different textures of

Group Activity.

raised beds and paving complement his plants, which have been chosen for year-round interest and variety. Raised beds need a lot of watering, but this gardener finds it easier with a lightweight watering can with a long spout.

Gardens unfold in many different ways, some at random, filling out with the seasons, some in stops and starts depending on budgets, others with controlled precision. Whichever way, a little planning can be helpful in assessing the potential of a site and in making those mistakes on paper rather than in the garden.

It is a very good idea to get to know the garden before making any drastic changes. You could draw a rough plan of your garden and mark in all the existing features including things like the best views or eyesores. Then draw up a list (one to ten) of all the things you would like to do or grow in your garden and your resources, such as time, skills, tools, money and so on. You can then

fill in what you would like to do on your existing site plan. Here is a checklist to help you:

- Location, with respect to access, ease of supervision, visibility from indoor day activity areas, proximity to water and electricity facilities.
- Size. Remember the most successful gardens are not necessarily the largest. Use what you have imaginatively and intensively.
- Aspect, warmth and shelter, degree of sun. Is there a need for extra shade or shelter? Many elderly people are very sensitive to changes in temperature and light – a comfortable outdoor environment is essential.
- Security. Can the garden be made secure to prevent easily confused people from wandering? Is there a need for protection against vandalism?
- Slope. A level site is best although not essential. Slopes or steps may be incorporated for therapeutic purposes.
- Soil – depth, fertility, drainage, pH. Do not despair if it seems unfavourable: soil can be im-

proved, plants can be chosen with extra care, containers can provide additional growing space.

- Existing planting, hard surfaces, walls, fences, garden features. How healthy or stable are they? Are they in the right place? Are they worth keeping?
- Consider when the garden will be used: every day, all year round, weekdays only, evenings only, fine summer days only, only at holiday times?
- Choose non-slip, non-reflective paving materials, and consider the merits of various 'safe' play surfaces (hard and soft) and of using different surfaces and materials for different purposes.
- Steps may or may not be appropriate, but gentle ramps, no steeper than 1:15, may be needed.
- Include plenty of handrails, grips and other support aids where necessary.
- Make sure pathways and hard-surface active play areas are wide or big enough for easy manœuvrability, considering children with walking aids or wheeled toys, or with balance problems.
- Avoid sudden unexpected changes in the direction of pathways.

- Water supply: put in standpipes, particularly near groups of containers or raised beds liable to dry out readily. A wall-mounted hose reel on a bracket next to the tap will be invaluable, especially if fitted with an adjustable spray nozzle. A network of trickle or seep hoses may also be useful.
- Wildlife potential: make the most of this and aim to improve it!
- Planning regulations: check them out.
- Proximity of neighbours: will extra screening be necessary to reduce noise?
- General facilities: washing line, barbecue and picnic area, summerhouse, patio, mothers' and toddlers' area, group or individual seating, hammock, area for swingbed.

Weeding and bending ... you don't have to face them for ever!

Weeds compete with and often choke the plants the gardener wants to grow. Possibly the easiest way of control is to smother them with ground cover plants. This is particularly effective where cultivation is difficult under trees, on banks or at the back of large borders. Because perennial weeds such as dock, dandelion, ground elder and

ALL I said was — "How's the garden these days?"

couch grass compete very successfully with ground cover plants, it is best to dig them out before planting begins. These weeds can be killed with contact weedkiller, but several applications are usually necessary. Make sure that the soil is thoroughly prepared with the addition of well-rotted farmyard manure, or peat and a base fertilizer such as Growmore or bone-meal. Carry out your planting in autumn or during a mild spell in winter unless your plants are container-grown, and you will find that they make rapid growth and soon fill up the open spaces between them. Once established, they will require little attention.

The choice of ground cover plants depends upon the soil, aspect and site. Some varieties do well in one type of soil and fail completely in another. Most heathers, for example, like acid soil although *Erica carnea* will grow in most soils, even those that are quite chalky. Visit your local library to get clued up on plant preferences.

Some areas of the garden may not lend themselves too readily to the use of ground cover plants, however. For example, in a rose garden or in a vegetable patch the cover plants would compete too actively for nutrients and water. In these situations it is a good idea to mulch with forest bark, spent hops, mushroom compost or a 5 cm. (2 in.) layer of peat. This layer on top of the soil will not only suppress weeds but also conserve moisture in drought conditions.

Putting things at the right height

When working at any job most people will raise the level of work to a convenient height. Indeed, most gardeners do this when growing pot plants in a greenhouse by using benches or staging, and it can also be achieved outside by the use of containers and raised beds.

The most convenient height for working from a seated position is that of a low table, about 75 cm. (2 ft. 6 in.) high. Most garden centres sell a whole range of containers at this height – half barrels, plastic tubs and wooden boxes. But don't forget to make full use of unwanted containers which other people may discard. Old fibreglass water tanks, for example, cut in half and painted with white exterior paint look as if they were designed specifically for growing plants in. Plastic

cooking oil drums can have the top cut off and be treated in much the same way. Cracked sewage pipes can look delightful painted and planted with trailing ferns or ivies, and an enamelled sink looks a hundred years old if covered with a mixture of cement and peat before being planted with alpines or rock plants.

Either choose the containers to suit the plants that you want to grow, or choose the plants to suit the containers. Large shrubs or fruit bushes require deep containers, while alpines are happy in shallow troughs which can be raised on brick piles. Good drainage is essential for either so place crocks over the drainage holes and add 5 cm. (2 in.) of stones or rubble. The nutrient supply in a soil-based compost such as John Innes Potting No. 2 will outlast that of a peat-based compost, be cheaper to buy or make, but will be far heavier. If you use ordinary garden soil, add peat to help with water retention, and sharp sand or grit if the soil is heavy.

Planting ideas

Aim at a garden that is full of sensory stimulus all year long. Make your garden manageable: avoid large areas of high-maintenance planting if you haven't the time to look after them.

- Plants with interesting textures, e.g., the felty leaves of *Stachys lanata*; the furry catkins (within easy reach) of *Salix lanata*; the strange feel of a mop-headed *Hydrangea*; the papery bark of *Betula jacquemontii*; the highly polished trunk of *Prunus serrula*; the ferny foliage of *Acer palmatum dissectum*.
- Bold foliage shapes, e.g., the huge-leaved ornamental rhubarb, *Rheum palmatum atropurpureum*, or glossy palmate leaves of *Fatsia japonica*; the stately *Angelica*; the sharp, spiky outlines of the hardy palms; the giant *Verbascum thapsus*.
- Unusual buds or flowers, e.g., the *Arisarum* (mousetail plant), *Antirrhinum* (snapdragon), *Allium christophii* (with football-sized flower heads); *Impatiens glandulifera* (giant balsam), *Escholtzia* (Californian poppy), *Magnolia* spp.
- Plants for drying, for use in indoor craft activities – many and varied.
- Interesting seedheads, e.g., *Lunaria* (honesty),

Nigella (love-in-a-mist), artichoke, pampas grass, *Eryngium*; ornamental maize, teasel.

- Nodding flower heads or fluttering leaves, e.g., quaking grass, Solomon's seal, *Dicentra*; aspen.
- Plants with strange, contorted stems, e.g., *Corylus avellana* 'Contorta', *Salix matsudana* 'Tortuosa'.
- Plants of particular value to wildlife such as birds, small mammals, insects; spring or summer meadows; bog or water gardens.
- Tiny plants, raised off the ground in tubs or troughs for easier viewing and minimal risk of damage; alpines, dwarf bulbs, miniature 'landscapes', miniature roses, tufa gardens.
- Fruit trees (on dwarfing rootstocks) as cordons or espaliers; cane fruit or bush fruit (trained for easy picking); filberts, crab apples – fun to pick and to use.
- Plants with a strong fragrance, e.g., *Philadelphus*, *Daphne*, *Hyacinthus*, honeysuckle, *Nepata*, *Phlox*; and with aromatic foliage, such as many herbs; 'Mediterranean' plants; *Geranium* spp, *Eucalyptus* – the list is endless!
- Brightly coloured flowers with simple and

Aim at a garden that is full of sensory stimulus all year long.

---

easily recognized daisy-like blooms that are good for cutting, such as *Chrysanthemum maxima*, *Rudbeckia*, *Gaillardia*, *Doronicum*, *Pyrethrum*.

- Plants with 'bite-sized' fruits, e.g., alpine strawberries, blackberries (thornless), cherry tomatoes.
- Unusual, decorative vegetables, e.g., ornamental kale, ruby chard, red lettuce, pink-flowered beans, purple-podded beans, sweetcorn, yellow tomatoes, broccoli 'Romanesco', spaghetti marrow, ornamental gourds and squashes; cut-and-come-again salads – edible bonus!
- Plants to supplement lunches; attractive ideas for children's bedrooms; for presents to be given away; to be sold.
- A small 'secret' garden, hidden away and laid out and managed entirely by children. Encourage them to choose plants that are easy to

grow and handle, have plenty of appeal, a long flowering season, and that can be used later: for drying, for instance.

- A 'fun' container garden, with plants set in a whole range of household and industrial containers of all shapes, sizes and dimensions.

A note of caution

A number of plants are poisonous to varying extents, depending on the dosage. In some cases, it is only part of the plant that is toxic, such as the root, the seeds or the leaves. In other cases, the whole plant is dangerous. Some plants can cause death, others may trigger vomiting, asthmatic attacks, skin irritation or minor allergies.

Some people, particularly those on certain types of medication, are especially sensitive to plants that may be quite harmless to others. It is wise to anyone planting a garden for children to find out about poisonous plants in order to judge the level of risk considered acceptable and to warn children against eating parts of *any* plants in the absence of adult supervision.

The hands of experience.

Down to basics

---- TWO ----

Hard outdoor surfacing

Here we take a hard look at what people actually walk on, or their wheelchairs spin along on, in the garden.

First of all, a word of advice – don't decide in a hurry. Avoid the temptation of saying yes to sharing a cheap load of gravel with a next-door neighbour; think about which material or combination of materials to use and how best to use them. Other points include:

- The needs and preferences of the people who will use the surfacing. Find out by involving them directly in the discussions from the beginning where possible.
- The surfacing function. Probably this will be to provide, first and foremost, a safe, firm and comfortable surface suitable for light use by pedestrians (whether fully or semi-ambulant), wheelchair users or those in other light-wheeled vehicles. It may also be necessary to provide areas of deterrent paving, to indicate possible hazards or as direction guides.
- How much money you have to spend. Remember that as well as the amount needed for materials, time and labour costs money; delivery and site preparation costs may have to be included too. The cheapest initial solution may prove in the long run to be the most expensive.
- The range of materials available.
- Aesthetic considerations. Design to blend in with the styles and materials of adjacent buildings and garden features where possible.

- Labour skills and equipment needed to lay the surface. Satisfy yourself that any cheap labour offered will be well managed and able to do the job effectively. Different materials require different skills.
- Time available! Some types of surfacing take longer to plan, acquire and install than others. Some cannot be laid in unfavourable weather conditions. Time often costs money.
- Suppliers. Investigate local ones first. Check delivery arrangements and the minimum size of load available. Obtain several quotes before deciding which to accept.
- Don't forget the site preparation that will be needed. This will vary with the material used and with local site conditions. Foundations, a sub-base, and adequate drainage provision must all be considered. Watch out for nearby tree roots that could cause problems early on or later.
- Slopes and edges. Pay particular attention to how you will deal with them. Edges are equally important, to define paved areas for safety reasons and to contain the surface material.

Who needs what?

1. Ambulant or semi-ambulant disabled people

This group may include people who have had strokes or amputations; who are affected by forms of arthritis or rheumatism; who have respiratory or heart conditions; or those who are frail and unsteady on their feet.

The prime requirement is for a surface that is level, firm, well textured to provide good grip and also one that drains well. Uninterrupted passage must be provided throughout, free from obstacles such as raised manhole covers, unexpected kerbs, occasional steps or overhanging branches. Sudden changes of direction and steep gradients are not recommended.

Steps should be surfaced with non-slip treads, be of uniform height, comfortably wide and deep enough to support a whole foot and any ancillary support aid easily. Handrails are essential, both to provide extra support and define step edges for extra safety.

2. Wheelchair users

The main priority is to provide smooth, uninterrupted and level surfaces to allow for free wheel movement with minimum effort.

Textured surfaces are less important than for ambulant disabled people, except on ramps, where they are essential for extra grip.

Kerbing is particularly important to prevent wheels from inadvertently leaving pathways. Choose chamfered, rather than sharp-edged, kerbing – it is kinder on the feet if accidentally bumped into.

Steps and steeply sloping ramps should not be considered unless alternative access is provided. Long stretches of shallow ramping are best designed with rest platforms incorporated. Ramps are best sited in open, sunny locations, where frost and ice will not be as persistent as in shady locations. Do provide adequate space for passing places, to allow people to walk comfortably alongside chairs and to permit easy turning and manœuvrability where these are necessary, such as at corners or at either ends of a ramp.

3. Visually impaired people

This group includes people who are partially sighted (i.e., those who have short or long sight, or 'tunnel' or peripheral vision only) as well as those who are completely blind. Many visually impaired people are also elderly.

Main requirements are that the materials chosen are firm and well laid, non-slip and dry, for maximum safety.

A wet path is not only a slippery path, it may be uncomfortably dazzling in bright sunshine, reducing residual vision considerably, so good drainage is vital.

Light-coloured, reflective surfacing materials can also cause glare, particularly if the garden area lies near buildings made of materials with similar properties. Choose non-reflective surfacing or provide partial shading.

Raised kerbs at path edges are preferred by some and actively disliked by others. They can be useful for people with canes, to tap along. If they are to be provided, however, make sure they are substantial, to reduce the risk of accidents.

Changes in the texture of surfacing (such as gravel to brick or paving stone), if laid with absolute accuracy to ensure they are level, are frequently easy to detect by visually impaired people through the soles of shoes or by a cane (if used). These can be planned to convey information concerning a change of direction just ahead or to guide people purposefully into a garden.

The colour of surfacing materials should be carefully chosen. Background colours are best kept neutral but contrasting colours can be used as markers to warn those with some residual vision of hazards or special features. The edges of steps, gateways, corners or a main circulatory pathway can be made more obvious in this way. White or yellow colours are generally easily recognized.

4. Mentally handicapped people

Many mentally handicapped people are physically able and well-coordinated. Common-sense principles therefore apply, the main aim being to provide firm, safe and non-slip surfacing.

This is all the more important where difficulties in physical co-ordination and balance are experienced and ample room for free movement becomes essential.

Since mental handicap may also be associated with other impairments such as epilepsy, deafness or cerebral palsy, the needs of these will have to be borne in mind too.

Construction of a concrete/aggregate path. Good multi-purpose surface, but this example is too narrow and winding for wheelchair users. Photo courtesy of the 'Cement & Concrete Association'.

Above all, aim at a safe, uncluttered environment that is easy to interpret and move around in and avoids confusing or conflicting messages.

5. Children

Clearly, planning hard surfacing for children must directly relate to the particular nature of their disabilities in the same way as for adults.

Remember though that it may be especially important to provide wide, straight thoroughfares ideal for wheeled toys and self-propelled vehicles to zoom up and down on, and to provide plenty of room for accompanying adults and group play.

The provision of specialist areas of soft surfacing, such as chipped bark or safety play materials, may be advisable either throughout or in certain areas, especially for very young children and those with profound handicaps.

This group of children benefits enormously from the stimulus value of different types of soft surfacing, which could also include ground cover carpets of contrasting, fragrant or brightly coloured plants.

What is there to choose from?

Contrary to what one might expect from a cursory look at surburban gardens, the choice of materials available for hard surfacing is in fact very wide: it's a question of knowing where to look. Most garden centres stock a relatively restricted range, though there are exceptions – mainly the larger ones or those with specialist patio franchises attached. Once you have thought about the preliminary considerations above, however, you should have a good idea of what you are looking for and be prepared to make enquiries until you find it.

The following notes describe the main properties of the principal materials on the market and are intended to help you narrow your choice of alternatives to suit particular requirements.

In situ *concrete*

Note: Other forms of concrete used as surfacing include pre-cast concrete slabs and interlocking blocks.

Good points: excellent, firm surface, if laid well and textured for extra grip. One of the most flexible materials – can be easily moulded to any shape. Useful for curved paths. Relatively low cost, long-lasting, minimal maintenance. No loose particles to cling to footwear/wheels. Only DIY skills needed. Can be made up on site or bought ready-mixed. Wide colour range. Combines well with other contrasting materials. Can be smooth enough for wheelchairs or textured enough for semi-ambulant people.

Limitations: poor aesthetic appearance if used on its own over large areas. High glare risk unless mixed with other materials, used in coloured form or part-shaded by planting. (Can be painted with special colourant later, but risk of blotchiness.) Can't be laid in wet or very cold weather. Large areas require several hands, work takes time and needs careful advance planning.

Tarmac (asphalt)

Made from chippings, crushed stone or slag, raked into hot bitumen or tarmac base then rolled.

Good points: very firm surface if well laid. Good grip after rain. Non-reflective in bright sunshine. Appearance fairly good, particularly if surface dressed with quartz chippings. Very flexible. Available in red, green or black. Fairly easy to lay, by skilled amateur or professional, even in damp weather. Cost comparable to that of concrete, though cheap end-of-run loads may be available from local councils. Lorry delivery or DIY bags.

Limitations: can be cracked by tree roots and perennial weeds. Thorough consolidation and weed elimination beforehand essential. Must be laid within well-defined edges at correct thickness, otherwise breaks up easily. Damage from frost-heaving common – later patching up may be necessary. May become soft and sticky in hot weather, causing problems for wheelchair tyres, especially if narrow.

Paving

Good points: very wide range of types available – concrete paving slabs, stone or reconstituted stone pavers, interlocking, hexagonal or round pavers, simulated brick or pattern-pave slabs. Wide range of colours and surface textures to suit different purposes. Wide price range according to type and delivery costs. Unbranded concrete slabs cheapest but more costly than *in situ* concrete. Stone slabs most costly. Can be DIY laid, although interlocking pavers require more skill than plain slabs and need vibrating in. Simulated brick (e.g., herringbone, parquet or other patterns) easier and quicker to lay than brick, but pattern-pave (blocks textured to look like granite setts) more specialist.

Limitations: many older slabs and those with smooth ground finish too slippery for semi-ambulant people, especially when wet. Must be laid extremely level with minimum-width joints for efficient wheelchair use. Loose, uneven slabs treacherous. Lighter colours often too reflective in bright sun and after rain. Care needed to keep weeds down between slabs – brush dry cement over; use herbicides or boiling water, or hand weed. Cheaper versions can look stark over large areas – mix with other materials. Not as flexible as brick, but can be cut with angle grinder. May crack under weight of vehicles, though small unit interlocking pavers take weight well and don't creep. Particular care needed over sub-base preparation on clay soils.

Other comments: riven reconstituted stone good value. Simulated small setts difficult to lay evenly. Hexagonal slabs can't be mixed easily with other shapes. Round slabs often scarce but useful as stepping stones. Natural stone slabs vary enormously in price (with availability), also in quality. Surface finish difficult to guarantee, can be slippery.

Brick

Good points: wide availability of shape, texture, colour and price, depending on type. Extremely versatile, durable, minimal maintenance. Often very attractive, particularly when laid in co-ordinated patterns. Provides good, firm, non-slip surface if the right type, suitable for paving, is chosen and laid well. Useful for gradual changes in level or direction and for demarcating edges as contrast. Fast to lay – no delay during hardening period as for cement or tarmac.

Limitations: quality and performance varies with type of brick. Rough stocks and common household bricks not suitable – former often uneven and of variable shape, both types porous, neither frost-resistant.

Gravel

Good points: cheap, readily available, very flexible, easy to lay, good informal appearance and colour range, never slippery, drains easily. If right thickness, a good, all-weather surface for semi-ambulant people as walking-sticks can dig in for extra grip. Easy to take up and re-lay.

Limitations: unsuitable for wheelchairs, especially if thick. Even if well consolidated beneath and laid thinly, wheels may rut ground, producing uneven, poorly drained surface. Painful to fall on. Some maintenance needed (raking, weeding, removal of dead leaves). Needs good edging to avoid loss of gravel.

Cobbles

Good points: attractive, informal appearance, whether set random, coursed, in patterns or in loose piles. Cheap where materials at hand. Especially good in small areas near buildings – more intimate scale than pavers.

Limitations: can be slippery. Very uneven if poorly laid or laid with cobbles raised above concrete. Generally unsuitable for most physically disabled people.

Hoggin

Fine gravel or chippings (scalpings) set into binder matrix of clay.

Good points: informal appearance, cheap if available nearby, very flexible, good grip when evenly laid.

Limitations: must be laid on very well-prepared and compacted yet well-drained base. Ruts easily with wheelchair use. 'Walks' indoors and can be muddy. Good edges essential. Must be bought as consistent grade. Clay in the binder matrix is difficult to work with, particularly when it is compacting.

Bark

Good points: can form a relatively hard surface if laid onto firm foundations and maintained well. Grip properties good for ambulant people. Most attractive, particularly in rural setting. Porous. Non-reflective. Soft in event of accidents. Sensory value particularly useful for children and profoundly handicapped people.

Limitations: once laid, takes time to consolidate and then may rut easily beneath narrow wheels on slopes and corners. Expensive, regular topping-up needed. Good edging required. Short life, decomposes eventually. Some risk of honey fungus infection.

Epoxy-bonded resin aggregate

A non-slip, decorative surface applied to smooth materials such as concrete.

Good points: attractive. Several colours and grades of aggregate. Useful as contrasting material. Very safe, excellent grip and drainage properties. DIY kit form available.

Limitations: expensive. Takes about a day to harden.

Wood

Used in form of railway sleepers, decking or transverse sawn log sections.

Good points: attractive, rustic appearance, natural material. Looks particularly good in rural setting or near wooden buildings.

Limitations: short life, even when mature unwarped pressure-treated timber used, particularly in damp, poorly ventilated sites. Can be treacherously slimy and slippery in wet or icy weather. Risk of splinters. Must be well planed.

Other comments: more durable, rough texture of end-grain gives best surface. Redwood, cedar, cypress, second-hand timber and railway sleepers last longest, especially if laid on sound bed with perforated polythene sheeting beneath.

Crazy paving

Good points: cheap, useful way of using old paving slabs and odd bits of stone. Attractive, informal appearance. Gives even, firm surface if well laid.

Limitations: easy to lay badly using poor materials on poor foundations – breaks up readily. Must have good edging or deteriorates rapidly. Accurate cutting and laying demands precision.

THREE

What about lawns?

The subject of lawns is one that invariably evokes strong feelings in one direction or another. For some, the neat square of green velvet with hardly a daisy in sight becomes the epitome of gardening excellence, a veritable goal to strive towards. A well-kept lawn acts as a foil against which to set off seasonal displays of flowers and foliage and is an attractive feature in its own right. It is also a practical asset, providing the opportunity for all sorts of varied outdoor activities. However, there is another side to this story. Many elderly or disabled gardeners find the maintenance demands of their lawns to be a major source of worry, particularly at the height of the growing season, when grass grows fast and there are neighbourhood standards to keep up. Another common concern is that of access, some lawn surfaces being difficult or unsafe to walk on or to cross in a wheelchair.

This chapter sets out a number of suggestions to help solve some commonly experienced lawn difficulties. Full technical details can be checked out easily in some of the excellent books already available on the subject. A simple lawn care calendar is also included here, since much time and effort can be saved if maintenance operations are carried out at the right time of the year. We pass on some ideas and hints to make various practical lawn care tasks easier to carry out — particularly for those who have limited mobility or less strength than in days gone by.

*　　*　　*

Improving accessibility

A lawn with a spongy, uneven surface can only be of limited use to its owners. Indeed, anyone who has difficulty walking or who is wheelchair-bound will do their utmost to avoid it. In the interests of both healthy grass growth and the safety and confidence of users, a level, firm lawn surface is essential.

Access across the lawn can be improved by managing it correctly and by reinforcing its surface artificially to form stable areas or 'pathways'.

1. Management. Ideally, a lawn intended for use should be laid or sown on a firm, level surface. But what if you have inherited a lawn that has deteriorated through the action of wear and tear, successive frost-heaving and the accumulation of wormcasts and molehills? Do not despair! The careful use of a light roller will usually even out minor irregularities and firm grass roots. However, over-compaction of the soil and the waterlogging that accompanies this is a common cause of poor grass growth and subsequent moss invasion, particularly on heavy soils. Only if weather and soil conditions permit should you consider rolling your lawn.

A top-dressing of lawn sand, peat or loam, brushed in and levelled, can be a useful way of eliminating minor irregularities. To level larger bumps or hollows it may be necessary to carry out minor lawn repairs: cutting and rolling back the turf and removing or adding soil as necessary, before rolling it back down again.

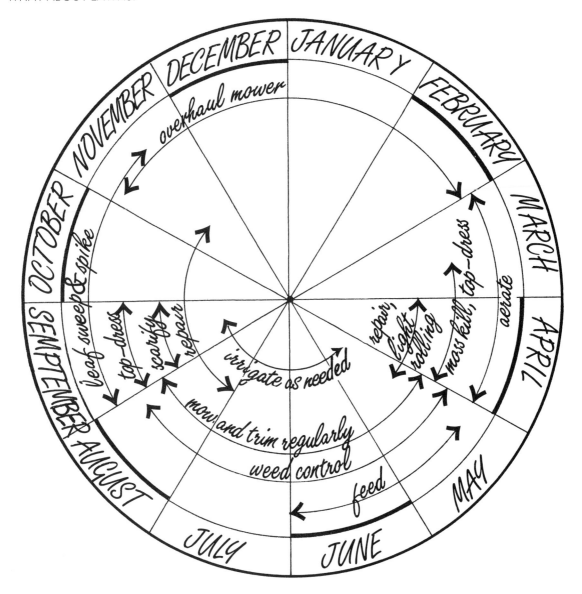

Note: The diagram is intended as a general guide only since local soil conditions, lawn type and seasons vary widely, thus affecting the exact timing of operations suggested. Months may vary in southern hemisphere.

2. Lawn reinforcement. If you want a tough, resilient lawn surface that you can get onto in most weathers, it might be worth considering reinforcing a part of the lawn to create, for example, a grassy pathway. This can be done by laying pre-cast paviors or house bricks in an open pattern, and allowing grass to grow in between them, to create a hidden path. Alternatively, semi-rigid artificial netting – which allows grass to grow through – can be laid to provide a firm footing, without affecting the look of the lawn. In all cases, this reinforcement allows weight to be more evenly distributed and lawn damage is minimized.

Scarifying and sweeping

Over time, most lawns tend to accumulate a surface mat of dead grass and moss, old clippings and ageing leaves, collectively known as 'thatch'. Vigorous raking or sweeping (scarifying) is an effective way of removing thatch, allowing water and fertilizers to reach grass roots more easily. It is best carried out in autumn when the turf thickens naturally. A traditional besom broom with a head made of twigs tied together works effectively as a scarifier. Somewhat lighter and equally useful is the spring-tined lawn rake designed specifically for the purpose. Light, tubular aluminium models with long handles are the easiest to use.

A wheeled leafsweeper – lightweight, easily pushed and with an easy-grip 'pram' handle – can be invaluable where large quantities of leaves are involved. A model with a light detachable bag allows the leaves to be carried with minimal effort to a nearby wheelbarrow, bonfire site or compost heap. For something cheaper and smaller, try one of the featherlight grabber-rakes or garden grabs, that save you having to bend and are useful for picking up all sorts of things from ground level.

Aerating (or spiking)

Heavily used lawns become compacted. This impedes the free passage of air and also results in poor drainage. Root development is hindered, which becomes particularly detrimental during drought periods. Lawns, especially those on heavy soils, need spiking at least once a year to improve aeration – preferably in autumn.

There are a number of ways of aerating a lawn. Small areas can be satisfactorily spiked using a garden fork. Traditionally, sports turf experts use hollow-tine forks which remove narrow plugs of turf when pushed into the lawn. The holes left are filled with lawn sand or a top-dressing. A simple version is available on the market, which has two hollow tines joined by a cross-bar, mounted on a long 'pram' handle. The tool can be operated easily without bending: simply hold on to the handle and press your foot on the crossbar to push the tines into the ground.

The amateur can also use a light rotary aerating machine, which is pushed along like a lawn mower. This requires some forward pressure, and a long-handled model is easier to use than a short-handled one. You can also carry out the job by purchasing spiked boards that fit easily onto shoes and, wearing these, walk up and down your lawn as systematically as possible...good leg action is required for this, though! Also, see home-made aerator in Chapter Eleven.

Weed control

Weeds are commonly defined as plants in the wrong place. Indeed, many people like a lawn to consist of lawn grasses alone, considering anything else present to be a weed, however slightly. Moss and broad-leaved lawn weeds can be killed by the use of a selective systemic weed-killer over the whole lawn or in 'spot' treatment. Many proprietary brands are available, suitable for use on lawns. Their systemic nature means that they are taken into the plants' transpiration system and hence work from the inside. It is therefore best to leave the lawn uncut for at least five days before application so as to ensure the maximum leaf area is available for absorption. Avoid hot dry days or rainy weather, which can both reduce the effectiveness of the herbicide. After absorbing the weedkiller, the broad-leaved plants often grow very fast, becoming blanched and twisted. Finally, after several weeks, they die.

It is best to avoid putting lawn clippings collected soon after treatment on the compost heap. Never be tempted to mulch plants with clippings from freshly treated lawns, as many harmful herbicidal chemicals are residual and remain active for months afterwards.

Wheeled distributors for granular fertilizer or weedkiller are particularly useful for people who walk with a stick.

'Spot' weeding of individual weeds can be carried out mechanically using a trowel, or chemically using a watering can and dribble bar or shield. However, the use of a 'weedwiper' glove, or a spot applicator in the form of a wick or impregnated stick at the end of a long handle, can save the need for lifting or bending and also allows for greater precision and accuracy.

A word of caution – when using liquid herbicides, always take every precaution to read the label and follow the directions given exactly. Granular herbicides can be much easier to handle and measure than liquid formulations. Finally, if all this still proves too much, then perhaps you should aim to create a summer floral lawn with a sward of colourful daisies, buttercups and yarrow. At least a clover-filled lawn rarely needs watering and stays green all year long.

Feeding

In a fairly rainy climate, where rainwater leaches plant nutrients down through the soil, all plants benefit from time to time from a boost of fertilizer. Grass is no exception. A good feed will strengthen and thicken it and improve resistance to drought, weeds, disease, moss and hard wear.

A light top-dressing fertilizer, high in nitrogen and perhaps mixed with grit, loam or peat, can be applied in spring, once the danger of frost has passed, to encourage leafy growth. In autumn, the fertilizer chosen should be relatively high in phosphates, to encourage root growth throughout the winter. This must be applied while the grass is still actively growing. The application of granular fertilizer using a wheeled mechanical spreader should give an even distribution of fertilizer at a pre-selected rate much more easily than if a similar fertilizer is spread by hand – even if the lawn is measured out in metre squares beforehand. These wheeled lawn spreaders are particularly useful for people who walk with a stick or who work from a wheelchair.

Watering

For most of the year, lawns do not need watering. However, occasional dry spells in spring or summer, especially in areas of light soil, may present a need for watering in order to prevent grass from dying back, thereby weakening the lawn. Avoid frequent light watering, which encourages shallow rooting, but also avoid heavy watering, which promotes moss and disease.

Small lawns are best watered using a hosepipe with an adjustable spray nozzle, whilst a sprinkler system is ideal for a larger area. Make sure you choose a system which is easy to set up and fit together, as well as to control – there are a number of different systems on the market.

Edging

A well-tended lawn can be considerably enhanced by neatly trimmed edges. Long-handled edging shears are the traditional tool for the job, but the slightly stooped position that they require for operation can easily induce backache after a short time.

There are tools on the market, however, that avoid this problem and can be operated easily when handled from an upright posture. One example has a non-slip rubber roller which can be pushed along the lawn edge while the attached rotating blades cut all overhanging grass quickly and efficiently. Electric edge trimmers, powered by rechargeable batteries, are another alternative. They can be pushed or pulled, and cut tight circles or straight lines with ease. One model has an operating handle which is roughly walking-stick shaped, allowing it to be managed easily with one hand, providing the user has good balance or a stick for support in the other hand.

If you prefer to kneel on the ground (or a kneeling pad) to do your edging, there are a number of well-designed hand lawn trimmers on the market, some being easy to grip and operate using only one hand.

Mowing

If you have neither the strength, time nor interest to roll, spike, scarify, brush, weedkill, water or feed your lawn, then it probably won't be top quality, but at least it will look like a lawn. Not so with mowing, for this is the one unavoidable lawn-care chore. Even if you don't notice grass growing around your feet, neighbours will. . . .

A push-along lawn edger can make lighter work than conventional long-handled shears.

Most of us know that mowing requires constant effort – particularly at the height of the growing season in the late spring and early summer, when grass can grow as fast as 10 cm. (4 in.) a week in favourable conditions. Indeed, most lawns will need cutting about 30 times a year. Here are some ways of making mowing easier:

● See that the shape and layout of your lawn is simple, preferably without sharply curved edges, island beds and specimen trees or shrubs to make mowing awkward. Overhanging branches that require you to duck beneath with the mower can be a nuisance or even dangerous. Aim for long runs up and down the lawn where possible – except of course where a hover mower is used from side to side.

● If you have a large area of lawn and limited strength, then don't mow it all at once. Stop before you feel tired and mow it in sections with breaks in between.

● Don't aim for a close-cropped ornamental lawn – they take more effort to mow and don't wear as well, so aim instead for a utility cut, perhaps 2.5 cm. (1 in.) high, which shouldn't need mowing more than once a week in summer.

● Electric mowers are generally lighter than petrol-driven mowers. Do take every precaution though to prevent accidents from happening. Use a circuit breaker at all times. Use an extension socket on a spike that can be stuck into the centre or the edge of the lawn, with spare cable coiled alongside it and paid out naturally as you mow up and down alongside, moving farther away from the socket.

FOUR

Raised beds

Talk to some people about gardening with disabled people and their eyes will suddenly light up – 'Aha, they do it in raised beds, don't they?' You can almost see the vision in their mind's eye of a sterile concrete box structure planted with a few lonely African marigolds for two months of the year. Well, it doesn't have to be like that . . . .

First of all, let's dispel two popular misconceptions.

Misconception A

Gardening with disabled people necessarily implies the use of raised beds.

Certainly, many people do find gardening much more comfortable if the soil surface is raised in some way, whether by a few centimetres or three-quarters of a metre.

This is particularly true for those who experience difficulty in bending or balancing or who have restricted mobility generally. Raising the soil surface can make all the difference between being able to garden at all and finding it out of the question. However, people's needs and abilities vary. Many, often those in wheelchairs included, actually prefer to garden at ground level – provided suitable lightweight, long-handled tools are available. Working at a straight-sided raised bed may be difficult for someone in a wheelchair who cannot lean forwards to reach the soil or cannot twist their spine to work sideways on.

So the key message here is to find out what the most comfortable gardening position is and to provide plants at the appropriate height, whether this means raising the soil level or not. Where a group of people of different needs and abilities are involved, it makes good sense to provide a range of growing surfaces at different heights, including some at ground level.

Misconception B

Raised beds are unusual and often unattractive garden features which have not been around for very long and which require special expertise to install and manage for use by disabled people.

This is not true! The growing of plants at different levels is by no means new or unusual. A border on top of a retaining wall or along a flight of shallow steps, or even in a window box, is as much a raised bed as is a temporary tub, a purpose-built planter or a growbag on a couple of breeze-blocks.

What do raised beds have to offer?

1. For many (but not all!) they considerably increase the opportunities for gardening by bringing both soil and plants within easy each.
2. Urban dwellers with tiny balconies or backyards may find that growing plants in raised beds or containers is the only way they can do gardening at all.

It makes good sense to provide a range of growing surfaces at different heights.

3. They can be useful ways of dividing a garden into distinctive areas, or of providing privacy.

4. In some gardens, the slope, soil depth, pH or soil fertility can cause major problems for successful plant growth. Raised beds can overcome such limitations.

5. A raised growing surface allows certain specimen or trailing plants to be displayed to maximum effect.

6. Mobile containers can be particularly versatile. Wheeled outdoors in summer, they can display semi-hardy plants or summer bedding. Wheeled into a greenhouse or conservatory in winter, they are ideal for winter bulb, herb or pot plant displays.

Where should raised growing areas be sited?

This deserves careful attention right at the beginning. Raised beds in the wrong position are of little value to plants or people. Here are a few guidelines to bear in mind to minimize the risk of this happening in your garden:

- **Privacy.** Avoid 'goldfish bowl' sites by locating the garden away from public access routes where possible. A degree of seclusion can do much to foster confidence and relaxation and is particularly important in a busy, institutionalized setting.

- **Water supply.** This is essential, since containers and raised beds, particularly small ones, need frequent watering in dry weather. A standpipe, with provision for a wall-mounted hose reel alongside, is the best solution,

although overhead, seep hose or trickle irrigation may be worth installing too.

- **Access.** Provide safe access, preferably to all sides of the bed, using surfacing which is stable, level, non-slip and non-reflective. Well-laid paving slabs, pavoirs, setts, bricks or concrete may be suitable. Provision may need to be made for the free passage of wheelchairs, people with crutches or walking frames and for adequate turning or overtaking space. Any steps or ramps should be very shallow (maximum slope for wheelchairs 1:15), with handrails where needed.
- **Shelter, aspect, shade.** Site the beds to take advantage of any existing shelter or shade, or provide shade as necessary. Avoid

Raised beds can be a beautiful and practical improvement to a garden but only when well designed and built as part of the whole garden plan. A poorly designed and constructed specimen can be a liability when it comes to selling your house!

Poor growing conditions such as a steeply sloping site, shallow or infertile soil or other site difficulties can be overcome with the help of raised beds or containers.

heavily shaded, cold or draughty situations which may limit plant growth and discourage active use of the beds. Minimize any uncomfortable glare from excessive areas of hard surfacing in bright sunshine by careful planting, sceening and choice of hard surface materials. Remember that people normally unaccustomed to being outdoors often burn easily and that a common side-effect of some modern drugs is increased photosensitivity of the skin.

- **Accessibility** to other living and working areas. Generally, see that raised beds are sited within easy reach of such areas, to allow ready access to shelter and cloakroom facilities.

Now to the details...

- **Dimensions.** It is not possible to recommend standard heights, widths and sizes, since individual requirements vary so widely. But certain guiding principles are always valid.

  Some people are more comfortable working at relatively low beds, or sitting down, possibly in a wheelchair, whereas others prefer to work at elbow level, standing up or leaning against the bed. Others require beds at several heights in order to minimize undue fatigue in any one part of the body. Bear in mind that low beds generally have more visual appeal and can be enjoyed by more people than high beds. Remember that gardens intended for use by several people should include a variety of beds at different heights, including some at ground level.

  The width of beds should also be governed by the gardeners' abilities. Ensure always that all parts of the beds are within comfortable reach, taking available tools into account. Naturally, beds accessible from two or more sides can be up to twice the width of those reached from one side only, or even wider if there is some permanent planting in the middle.

- **Seasonal or permanent?** Make sure that beds which will be moved indoors or into a glasshouse in winter are small and light enough to carry, and fitted with handles or mounted on wheels or castors. Mobile units allow the growing of a wide range of less hardy plants.

- **Footholes and knee-space.** These can be designed in for extra comfort and access for those who have to work at beds facing

The staggered face of this raised bed allows the gardener to stand comfortably, leaning close to the bed with feet facing forwards. The curved coping of non-abrasive material is comfortable to reach across and is extended in some places to provide leaning or resting slabs. The varied height of the bed walls act as a guide for visually handicapped gardeners as do the tactile changes created by mixing different building materials. These features look good too!

forwards. The three main ways of providing them are to:

a. Extend the upper part of the bed as a cantilever.

b. Design the bed like a manger or table top.

c. Build the base of the bed narrower than the top.

- **Extra supports.** These are particularly useful for those with limited balance. Design them as unobtrusively as possible. Think about providing:

a. Handrails or handgrips sited appropriately.

b. Seating, possibly built into part of the edge of a bed or provided in the form of a wide stretch of strong coping.

c. A wide stretch of coping or sloping kerb for easy leaning or support.

d. Leaning or slumping posts, judiciously placed near the bed. Try and incorporate them naturally into another structure such as an archway or pergola.

● **Shape of the bed.** Design the shape of the bed to allow the gardener with limited mobility to work to either side as well as in the front with the minimum of effort. An L-shaped curved bed may allow this, as will carefully designed indentations. Some building materials are clearly more flexible in this way than others.

For visually handicapped gardeners, use strong contrasting colours in the design, and also different surface textures or construction materials at strategic reference points (such as at corners or regular intervals along the length of the bed).

● **Construction materials.** Many are available but before making your choice think about:

1. Stability – safety is crucial!

2. Durability.

3. Construction skills required.

4. Cost.

5. Maintenance.

The most appropriate materials for raised beds are often:

a. *Stone.* Prepared walling or natural stone, laid dry or using mortar. May be a very high- or very low-cost alternative, often depending on availability. Choose local stone where possible. Skilled labour required for construction. Foundations needed.

b. *Brick.* Durable, strong, low-maintenance. Construction requires skills. Foundations needed, also provision of damp-proof course and lining of walls against house walls. Engineering or hard stock bricks give most professional finish but can be extremely costly. Domestic bricks are cheaper but porous, so must have coping of hard stock bricks. Use engineering bricks as footings to provide damp-proofing. Good range of colours and unit sizes available.

Containers at a variety of heights which could be tended from a wheelchair or with long-handled tools. Photo courtesy of 'Bradstone Garden Products'.

c. *Precast units*, e.g. concrete, fibreglass, reconstituted stone. Cheaper than brick or stone, except in self-assembly kits. Visual appeal varies. Less adaptable than brick or stone.

d. *Wood.* Very versatile and adaptable – railway sleepers, strong floorboards, wooden posts, split logs, round wood, telegraph poles. Ideally, should be pressure-treated. Buy ready-treated or, if not possible, paint, preserve and line the timber.

A trellis offers protection from north winds and support for climbers and shrubs growing in the raised bed and for cordon fruit trees planted at the side of the bed. Indentations in the container break up the line and improve access to the growing area or provide a welcome spot for a seat. A tiered effect is created by a small peat bed within the raised garden, providing an opportunity to vary the type of planting. Evergreen shrubs are planted in the least accessible parts of the bed but all other areas are easily reached from one side.

e. *Peat blocks.* Useful, particularly for beds for lime-hating plants. Cheap, minimal construction skills needed. Easily damaged, but blocks replaceable. For longest life, build bed in shade or semi-shade and keep blocks damp. May last up to ten years, particularly where blocks become bound together by plant roots.

● **Soils, compost, drainage.** Remember that plants growing in containers or raised beds are more vulnerable to moisture stress and nutrient deficiencies. The soil or compost used for raised areas must, therefore, be of adequate fertility and depth for the plants selected and provision must be made for supplementary feeding and irrigation where necessary. Free drainage of water from the beds is important. Provide it by ensuring that there are drainage holes at the base of any containers used and that several inches of coarse-grade material are laid before soil is added. Beds standing on solid bases will need drainage holes in the sides.

Lastly, do not forget that during the first year after planting, the soil level in the bed or container will settle and need topping up. It is wise to plant annuals only in the first season.

FIVE

Growing in containers

Do you only have a small garden or a balcony on which to grow plants outside? Do you have limited mobility, or difficulty in bending or reaching the soil from a sitting position?

One solution could be to use containers. Here are some of the benefits – and drawbacks – of gardening in containers, the range of containers that are readily available and some of the more unusual containers that can be used.

Containers are useful because:

- They can be used in a small space for added interest.
- You can put them anywhere – on the windowsill, by the back door, on the balcony or patio as well as around the garden.
- They are movable – you can arrange them in different groups and take delicate plants indoors for protection. Some can be mounted on trolleys or castors for easy moving.
- They are very adaptable – you can create any soil condition you require – from marsh to alpine – and position them in sun or shade.
- They can be arranged in groups and at different heights – for vertical gardening – and you can find a working height that suits you and makes the most of any space.
- They are versatile – you can change the plants throughout the year for maximum interest every season. You can also use them for vegetable growing.

- They are small areas for easy maintenance although they do require more watering and feeding than border soil.
- They come in very many shapes, sizes and colours.

However:

- Watering is important – clay containers dry out more quickly than those made of other materials. A gel is available which can be mixed with growing mediums to improve moisture-retaining qualities.
- As with house plants, guard against over-watering.
- Food for plants in containers gets used up so they need regular feeding – preferably on a little-and-often basis with liquid feeds.
- Weather conditions can be a problem with the containers, e.g., hard frosts may crack clay containers and damage the roots of plants, especially those in clay and plastic.

When buying a container, remember:

- The style and shape can complement other containers when grouping them for display.
- The style and shape can complement the plants to be grown.
- The size of the container will restrict the size of the plant. This can be useful for keeping

Containers can be mounted on trolleys or castors for easy moving.

some of the larger trees and shrubs to a manageable size.

● You have to get the container home! This is particularly important with larger containers. However, ask your shop or garden centre if they have a home delivery service and, when doing so, make sure of any charges made for the delivery.

What are containers made of?

There is a whole range of materials from which containers are made. There are merits and limitations on all these materials and these are laid out below.

Where to get them

Most garden centres stock a whole range of containers made of all the different materials mentioned above. This is particularly true of the larger garden centres and those attached to the DIY superstores. There are also a large number of manufacturers of containers, many of whom advertise in the gardening press.

There are a few unique containers that are worth mentioning separately. These have proved particularly useful for those who can't bend or who garden from a sitting position.

The Pyramid Garden

Made of a robust 'A'-shaped wood and alloy frame, the unit supports up to eight containers that give up to double the growing area on which it stands. The pyramid planter is useful indoors or out, though care must be taken when watering indoors, in case of spillage. A special model has been designed for people in wheelchairs. (See overleaf.)

	+	−
Plastic and polypropylene	Light, cheap, variety of sizes, shapes and colours. Some can imitate stone.	Can look cheap. Can deteriorate in the sunlight (go brittle).
Fibreglass	Lightweight.	Expensive. Can expose dangerous 'splinters'. Can be unattractive.
Clay and pottery	Large variety. Look good.	Can be heavy. Can crack in cold weather. 'Designer' items can be expensive.
Stone	Can blend with hard surfaces. Natural look.	Very heavy and difficult to move. Can be expensive.
Reconstituted stone	As stone.	As stone, though less expensive.
Moulded concrete	As stone.	As stone, though less expensive. Can appear 'concrety'.
Wood	Durable 'rustic' look easy to make yourself. Half barrels are relatively cheap and look good.	Can rot. Needs revarnishing/ preservative treatment. Can be expensive.

The Pyramid Garden.

Two of the less expensive ranges

Prefertilized containers

Vert-i-Grow units are specially designed circular polypropylene containers in $\frac{1}{2}$-, 1- and $1\frac{1}{2}$-metre tall units. Each unit has 'planting windows' which can be opened or closed to suit the number of plants to be grown.

Each unit is supplied with a soil-less growing medium and sufficient fertilizer for a growing season. The Vert-i-Grow system has been successfully used to grow bedding plants, vegetables and many other plants.

Care must be taken to ensure the compost is well watered before opening the 'windows' for planting. When the plants are small further care must be taken when watering to avoid washing the compost out of the unit.

Lightweight

Erin Marketing Limited manufacture a range of very lightweight containers. They come in sizes up to 45 cm. (18 in.) diameter and are square, round, hexagonal or oblong (troughs). Although they are made of recycled newspaper mixed with bonding agents and resins, they can last up to four years with careful handling. They are available from garden centres.

Home-made or unusual containers

If you cannot afford to buy containers, then why not make them, or look around for things to plant up? Anything that will take compost and the plants you want to grow will provide you with an unusual feature.

Old oil drums or chemical containers, paint tins, boots, lavatory pans, cisterns, stacks of tyres, tea chests, boxes, etc. Old sinks provide a particularly good container in which to grow alpines.

Planting up containers

Whatever containers you are using, whether bought, made or unusual, care must be taken with the planting up to get the most benefit out of your eventual display.

With used or unusual containers, make sure that they are clean; wash out any old compost, chemical or paint residues. If needed, treat the container with preservative (wood) or paint it to disguise its original use. Tea chests look good if they are painted matt black. If using paint or pre-servative, check the manufacturer's instructions to ensure it won't damage plants.

To help prolong the life of wooden containers – particularly the flimsier types – you can line them with thick black polythene.

Unusual containers – as with all containers, they can be arranged in different groups.

Deciding what you want to grow in the container will tell you the growing conditions you will need to create. Unless you are creating a bog garden, the container must have drainage holes. If not, the compost will become saturated and stagnant, killing the plants.

Having created drainage holes, you must find ways of avoiding the compost being washed out of them! This is done by placing a layer of stones or crocks (pieces of broken clay pots) in the base of the container. Over this rough drainage material, place a layer of finer stones or shingle.

The depth of drainage material will depend on the depth of the container but, as a rule of thumb, it should be about one-sixth of the total depth.

Which compost do I use?

This, too, will depend on the plants chosen. A general peat-based potting compost will do for most plants and has the added benefit of being light in weight. For containers with more permanent shrubs or trees, use a John Innes No. 3 compost. More specialist compost mixes, e.g., for alpines, cacti and acid-loving plants (ericaceous compost), etc., are available from most garden centres.

When planting up containers, take care not to group the plants too closely. The plants will grow and can get overcrowded. You should always think of the eventual size of the plant so that the container won't end up looking – or being – top-heavy. As there is a very wide selection of plants that will do well in containers it is not worth providing a plant list here. Instead, refer to the many gardening books which list plants for containers.

Finally . . .

To help give height to your display of containers, why not use a wooden stepladder? Painted matt black, this provides an excellent feature on which to stand smaller containers. These can be positioned on the steps and, if planted correctly, will provide a cascade of colour from top to bottom.

SIX

Getting straight – the garden shed

As most disabled or elderly gardeners will need to make frequent journeys between the garden shed and greenhouse or garden, its siting is of prime importance. It is best positioned with the doors facing the greenhouse and with a level paved or concrete area of about 1.5 m. (4 ft. 6 in.) square in between. As with the greenhouse, good access is essential, so ensure that the door is at least 75 cm. (2 ft. 6 in.) wide and that there is no barrier at ground level. Chalet or summer-house-type sheds often have wide double doors and may be more suitable for wheelchair gardeners – especially if they intend carrying lapfuls of tools or seed trays about. Wooden, prefabricated floors which are supplied by the shed manufacturers may necessitate a ramp of about 5–7.5 cm. (2–3 in.) in height at the top end; alternatively it may be possible to sink the floor into the ground. In this case it is essential that the wood is pressure-treated with a good preservative, as it will otherwise rot rapidly.

To minimize accidents the garden shed should be as large and uncluttered as possible. Preparatory work such as sowing seeds in trays, potting up and taking cuttings should be done in this shed so that the greenhouse is kept free for its real purpose – growing plants. This means that all the tools need to be stored carefully in racks on the walls with consideration given to safety, and to the limited reach of some handicapped people. Racks with protruding hooks or nails present a danger to gardeners who may have poor balance, unless they are positioned above head height.

Magnetic bars are available which provide excellent storage for small metal tools such as knives, screwdrivers, etc. Wheelbarrows need a lot of turning space in a shed and are best stored elsewhere, perhaps in a car-port or veranda.

Ideally, there should be plenty of cupboards with open fronts or sliding doors. These need to be within reach of the gardener, but it is essential that the one used for storing fertilizers and pesticides is kept locked, as it may otherwise be accessible to children.

The work bench needs to be firm and strong, but this need not exclude the use of a folding design with gate legs. If the bench is more than 60 cm. (2 ft.) wide the back may be difficult to reach and clean, resulting in poor plant hygiene. The height of this bench is a matter of personal preference, but many wheelchair gardeners find 75 cm. (2 ft. 6 in.) to be about right.

It is a convenience to keep the potting compost immediately next to the work bench. Pull-out boards with holes to fit several sizes of pot allow filling and planting to be done with one hand, or, alternatively, the boards could be supported on the bench by a frame.

Ideally, the garden shed should be supplied with electricity for power and lighting. This will also enable a fan heater or tubular heater to be used for winter work and remove the temptation to use a paraffin stove. With so many metal tools around it would also be dangerous to use an open electric fire inside the garden shed, so use a fan or tubular heater instead.

A length of cane tied along the final half metre of hosepipe increases its range and directs the water more accurately.

...and what about watering?

Watering can all too easily become one of gardening's least enjoyable chores. Whether you have restricted mobility, are under orders to conserve energy carefully or are simply growing older, it's worth considering ways of reducing the demands it makes on precious time and effort:

- Minimize watering needs. For example, improve the soil structure, mulch plants, grow those that tolerate dry conditions, water only in early morning or evening.
- If you have the chance, make sure that all parts of your garden are within easy reach of a water supply. Distribute standpipes generously, and remember that containers and raised areas dry out more quicky than ground-level beds.
- Choose watering-cans that are light in weight, well balanced and have a long spout to minimize the shoulder and elbow action required in lifting and carrying them.
- Where you have a choice, use a hosepipe in preference to a watering-can. An adjustable spray nozzle fitted to a hosepipe can save much walking.
- Fit a lance to the end of the hose to increase its range and direct the water more accurately. A cheaper alternative is to tie a length of cane along the final half-metre or so of piping.

Minimize the effort of lifting with a lightweight, well-balanced watering can.

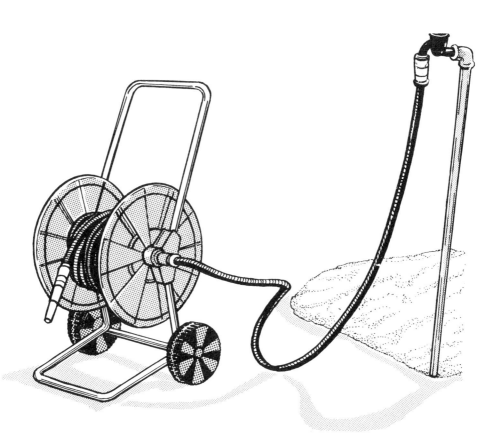

A hose reel on wheels makes it easier to reach all parts of the garden.

- The new 'lay-flat' hose attached to a cassette reel is particularly compact and easy to store, besides being less likely to trip up the unwary or visually handicapped gardener or hinder the wheelchair user.
- Indoors, keep plants on staging or shelving at a height which will allow comfortable watering.
- With careful management, automatic or semi-automatic watering systems in your greenhouse may well be worth the initial investment. Capillary systems (using sand, expanded clay or matting), trickle, overhead and drip watering systems can all be useful. Choose a system that suits both yourself and your plants.
- Try lining hanging baskets with offcuts of carpet underfelt this year. This holds moisture for a long time without waterlogging.
- Leaky watering-can? Pour some paint inside, swirl it round and leave it for a fortnight to set; it will seal any small holes.

SEVEN

Tools and how to choose them

Finding the right tools for the right job and the right person is as important as knowing how to use them properly.

Both factors play a decisive part in our enjoyment of gardening. Good posture makes gardening easier, bad posture can lead to lasting physical problems. Many gardeners have special needs, so here is a guide to choosing and using tools.

Some points to remember

First of all, remember that some ground rules of good posture include to keep your back as straight as possible; exert force from the knees (when lifting) and hips (when pushing), using the arms and shoulders as a secondary force.

- Choose lightweight tools wherever possible: tools with plastic, carbon fibre or aluminium handles are the lightest.
- Tools which are clean and oiled occasionally are easier to use and will last longer.
- Stainless steel tools offer less resistance to the soil and are easier to keep clean, but do not usually have a sharp edge.
- Use power tools – if you can cope with the weight: look out for cordless rechargeable ones (many tools are available for hire).
- With all gardening jobs try to do a little often. This will cut out the need for doing larger, more exhausting jobs.
- If necessary, reduce the need for cultivation by planting perennial plants and by mulching.

- Finally, remember that when you buy a tool it is essential that you get one that suits you. Never purchase a tool without having tried it out for weight, balance and suitability for the job you want it to do.

Do you have a back problem? Do you find it difficult or impossible to bend? Gardening can still go on. Indeed, the exercise will benefit your back provided you follow some simple rules.

Some hints on choosing tools that can be used without bending the back.

Digging. This is the most strenuous gardening activity anyone will have to do – particularly on heavy or stony soils. Try using a lightweight border spade or fork; or, for better leverage, choose long-handled spades or forks with 1.4–1.8 m. (4 ft. 6 in.–6 ft.) handles. The Wolf-Terrex autospade cuts out the need for bending.

Cultivating. This term used to mean cutting and chopping the soil by plough, tines or cutters, or the method of working peat, compost and fertilizers into the soil. Cultivators can be used as an alternative to digging, especially on light soils. The most useful tools are those with long, lightweight handles.

Hoeing. The easiest hoes to use are those that have a double action – they can be pushed and pulled. For maximum efficiency, hoes that have a

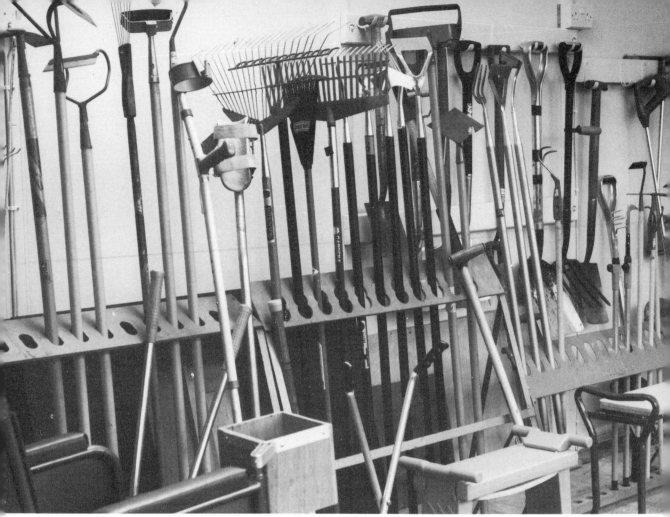

A whole range of tools is now available and many of them are light in weight.

fixed rather than swivel head need to be checked to make sure that the angle of the blade is correct for your height. The lighter the hoe, the less strain it will put on your back. However, a light hoe requires more pressure to cut through the soil.

Raking and collecting. 'Grabber-rakes' are useful for the two-in-one action of raking and picking up waste material. Alternatively use a lightweight rake and a 'grab'.

Watering. Using a watering-can places unnatural stress on the back. If possible, use a sprinkler sytem with a 'lay-flat' hose on a cassette reel (these are easier to manage and store than conventional reels), or a modern-style watering-can with a carrying bar. If you use a hosepipe there is a range of fittings to make watering easier. These include lance sprays with trigger controls to

extend your reach. In the greenhouse automatic watering systems can be used.

Wheelbarrows. If you use a conventional wheelbarrow always bend your knees, keep your back straight and lift by straightening your legs. Alternatively use a two-wheeled barrow with a 'walking-stick' or 'pram' handle that avoids the need to bend.

Lawn care. Always keep your lawn free of leaves and debris by raking and collecting. A wheeled lawn-sweeper or wheel rake takes a lot of heavy work out of sweeping and scarifying the lawn. Mowing cannot be avoided. Choose a light mower that has powered wheels thus cutting out the need for pushing; but make sure your mower is powerful enough for your garden.

If you have either a hand mower or one that does not have powered wheels, keep as upright as possible when pushing. Always push hover-

type mowers in a straight line and not in side-to-side sweeps.

Long-handled lawn shears or lightweight strimmers are useful for cutting grass in those difficult areas around trees and against walls or fences.

Pruning. A lot of pruning involves bending down or reaching up. If you find this difficult, tubular alloy pruners can be used for plants out of reach. Cut-and-hold secateurs are particularly useful for cutting and gathering flowers. Remember what a difference your choice of planting can make. Try to grow plants that require little or no pruning or those that put pruning within easy reach such as fruit trees grown as cordons, fans or espaliers.

Do you use a walking-stick or only have the use of one arm — perhaps because of injury or a stroke? Do you have a weak grip or find it difficult to hold tools because of arthritis, for instance? You can still go on gardening if you choose tools carefully or adapt the ones you've got.

Handle adaptations for one-handed use

Hand tools are easier to use one-handed than long-handled tools. But if you do need to use a heavier, long-handled tool, try this adaptation: attach two loops of strong leather (an old leather belt would do) to a wooden handle by means of screws (a metal handle needs to be drilled and the leather attached by a bolt and washers). Then attach a handle or auxiliary grip at a point where you can grip it (see figure opposite).

Some hints on how to tackle routine gardening jobs with one hand

Digging. Traditional digging may be out of the question if you only have one arm. Use minimum digging techniques or cultivating instead.

Hoeing. The easiest hoes to use are those that have a double action — they can be pushed or pulled.

Raking. Use the handle adaptation on long-handled rakes. Choose a lightweight rake or the wheel rake that takes all its weight on the wheels.

Wheelbarrows. Wheelbarrows with 'walking-stick' or 'pram' handles are designed to be used one-handed.

Lawn care. Choose a mower that is fairly light in weight and has powered wheels or roller. The safest type to use, however, is one with a 'walking-stick' handle. Sword-grip shears or cordless shears are designed to be used one-handed and can be used for edging or trimming small areas of grass, e.g., around trees and posts.

Pruning. Cut-and-hold secateurs are ideal for pruning if you only have the use of one hand. As their name suggests, these hold on to the cut material *as long as you keep the handles gripped.*

Tools that do not require a strong grip

It is essential to try out tools and find those that suit your grip. However, there are some general rules that will help:

- Find the lightest tools with the widest handles — these allow an easier grip (see figure opposite).
- When choosing shears or secateurs be sure to try a number of the same model — some springs may be looser than others, allowing an easier action.
- When holding tools, try to work for short periods at a time. The longer you grip a tool, the more the hand is likely to become 'fixed'. Vary the jobs you do so that different hand actions are required, giving the fingers more exercise.

Some simple adaptations to the handles of tools to give an easier grip

By enlarging the handles, tools become more comfortable and easier on the grip. Bind the handle of a tool with sponge and/or cloth. This can be built up in layers to suit your grip. There are also commercially available methods using sponge rubber or plastic foam which can be pushed over the handles of tools. Another method uses a two-part epoxy compound which is wrapped around the handle and, when gripped, moulds to the shape of your hand (see figure opposite).

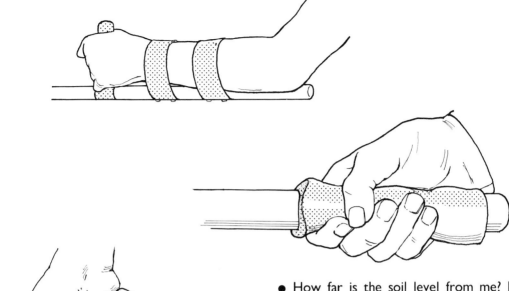

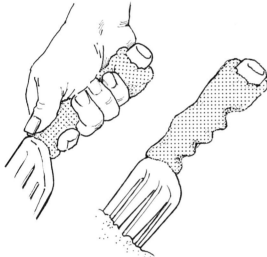

If you garden from a sitting position, either in a wheelchair or using a stool, bench or chair, there are plenty of tools available to you. Before choosing, though, ask yourself these questions:

- Do I need a large selection of tools? Will a few tools do most jobs?
- How can I transport tools to where I want to use them? The larger or longer the tools, the more difficult to transport.
- Can I reach all areas of ground from my sitting position? Areas out of reach could be planted with permanent subjects that require very little or no maintenance.

- How far is the soil level from me? Is it at ground level or raised? The closer the soil level, the shorter the length of tool required.
- Do I have much strength in my arms and shoulders? The less strength, the lighter the tools required.

Some hints about what to look for in tools to do the following jobs from a sitting position:

Digging. This is perhaps the most strenuous task for *any* gardener, particularly on heavy soils. Choose a lightweight border fork (sometimes referred to as a ladies' fork). Stainless steel is lighter and requires little maintenance.

Cultivating. The most useful tools for use from a sitting position are those with lightweight aluminium handles.

Hoeing. The easiest hoes to use are those that have a double action – the 'push–pull' type. Again, try the hoes out to see which suits you – look particularly at the working angle of the hoe from a sitting position.

Raking. A range of grabber-rakes is useful for gathering and picking up. There are also some *very* lightweight rakes available now.

Watering. If you use a hosepipe there is a range of fittings to make watering easier. These include lance sprays with trigger control, and various connections and nozzles.

A watering-can is difficult to transport by wheelchair. Look at ways of cutting down the need for hand watering by mulching or growing plants that tolerate drier conditions. Even better, use a sprinkler system if possible, with a 'lay-flat' hose on a cassette reel.

How to plant at ground level from a sitting (or standing) position using a long-handled trowel.
1. Dig a hole large enough to accommodate root ball.
2. Transfer plant from pot to trowel.
3. Slide plant from trowel into hole.
4. Refill hole using the blade of the Wolf-Double hoe LM and firm soil around plant using the prongs of the hoe.

Lawn care. A lawn is manageable from a wheelchair, provided:

a. It is dry and firm enough to take the weight of the chair.
b. A power mower is chosen that can be pushed at one's own pace (i.e., does not have powered wheels).
c. Care and suitable precautions are taken with mower cables.

Pruning. Fruit trees grown as cordons, espaliers and fans put pruning within easy reach of the seated gardener. Tubular alloy pruners can be used for plants out of reach.

Hand tools. Hand tools are very useful when working at raised beds where the soil is within easy reach. Some are available with longer handles for working at lower areas. Pay particular attention to how comfortable the handle is to grip.

EIGHT

What to look for in greenhouses

Greenhouses extend the enjoyment of gardening throughout the whole year. They are pleasant places to be in and invaluable working spaces in the winter months.

Access

The choice of greenhouse is extremely important to a handicapped person, the fundamental point being ease of access. Scouting through catalogues will show that only a few small, standard greenhouses have a doorway wide enough to allow a wheelchair or walking frame through. Sliding doors of at least 75 cm. (2 ft. 6 in.) wide with no barrier at ground level are vital.

Materials

The choice of materials depends on the individual, although future maintenance must be taken into account. An aluminium frame greenhouse requires no care, cedar wood requires very little, while painted wood needs regular attention. It is, of course, easy to fit extra handles to wooden doors if the ones supplied are at an inconvenient height.

*   *   *

Siting

Siting a greenhouse is important. If it is near the house it will be cheaper to lay on water and electricity, and less unpleasant getting to it in bad weather. But, ideally, the greenhouse should be sited to receive maximum light, which means being placed well away from overhanging trees and high walls, so a compromise may be necessary in the average garden.

If it is possible try to arrange the potting shed near the greenhouse, with facing doors, so as to cut down the travelling distance between the two.

Interior design

The path inside the greenhouse needs to be at least 75 cm. (2 ft. 6 in.) wide if the gardener is in a wheelchair. This path should be level, smooth and firm, preferably concrete or of paving slabs. So that the back of the staging can be easily reached, limit the width to 60 cm. (2 ft.). This will give a total greenhouse width of 2 m. (6 ft. 6 in.), and a minimum practical working length is 2.5 m. (8 ft.). Most wheelchair gardeners find the best height for staging to be about 60 cm. (2 ft.).

Heating

Electricity may not be the cheapest way of heating a greenhouse but it has many advantages,

particularly thermostatic control. Also the provision of electricity to a greenhouse could be
useful for the automation of shading, ventilation
and soil warming at a later date. A minimum temperature of 7–8° C (42–44° F) is sufficient to
grow many plants over the winter, although the
more tropical species will not tolerate this. In
fact, it is surprising how many plants will grow in
a totally unheated (or cold) greenhouse.

The two popular types of electric greenhouse
heater are tubular heaters and fan heaters. Fan
heaters tend to use more electricity but do cir-
culate the air and can be used to help ventilation
during the summer. Most manufacturers and
dealers will offer advice on the size of heater
required for the size of greenhouse.

Paraffin heaters are a good source of heat in
the greenhouse and are relatively cheap to use.
However, they do produce a lot of water vapour

1. Shade blinds on spring rollers.
2. Automatic heating controlled by rod thermostat.
3. Automatic watering.
4. Propagator with automatic temperature control.
5. Thermostatically controlled extractor fan.
6. Sliding door.
7. Tubular heater.

and condensation and can smoke unless the wick
is kept trim and well adjusted. The heater should
always be filled outside the greenhouse as spilt
paraffin contaminates soil and gives off harmful
fumes.

Ventilation

Greenhouses usually have windows for ventilation in the roof; the warm air rises, escapes through these when they are open and cooler air is drawn in through the door or side windows. Several firms market a simple expanding tube type of attachment which can be fixed to the ventilator. These will automatically open and shut the ventilator depending upon the temperature. Versions are also available for louvre panels. A pole with a hook on the end can enable a wheelchair-bound gardener to operate ventilators himself.

The most efficient type of ventilator is the thermostatically controlled extractor fan. These are easy to install and cheap to run, providing a continuous movement of air and reducing condensation. They are normally fitted to the gable end of the greenhouse.

Shading

Shading has two main functions. Firstly to stop the sun's rays from scorching the leaves, fruit, etc.; secondly to prevent too much radiant heat from entering the greenhouse and so keep its temperature to reasonable limits. But in addition some shading systems such as slats and blinds can be used to help keep the heat in on cold nights.

The best way to shade is by roller blinds which can be rolled up or down depending on the weather. Interior blinds are easier and cheaper to fit, but external ones take up no plant space. Inside blinds are operated by cords which can be extended for wheelchair users, while outside blinds are controlled by an electric motor.

The cheapest type of shading is to paint the outside of the glass with a special shading paint. This is a powder which is mixed with water and evenly applied. It can be rapidly removed in the autumn with a cloth. The disadvantage of shading paint is that it provides shading for the greenhouse whether the day is sunny or cloudy.

Watering

Correct watering is one of the most difficult things to achieve. If you lack strength or mobility in the arms but need to water manually choose a light plastic can with a long spout. Alternatively, tying the end of a hose to a cane or broom handle will extend the reach. Never try squirting the water by pinching the end of the hose as this leads to inconsistent watering and severe erosion of compost from the pots. It also tends to knock dry, and therefore light, plant pots over. Lances with control triggers are useful to avoid splashes which can spread fungal and bacterial spores.

Greenhouse pot plants can be watered automatically using capillary action or trickle irrigation. Perhaps the most efficient way is by using capillary matting laid on the floor of the greenhouse bench. The pots stand on it and only take up the water they need. A seep hose laid along the mats takes all the work out of it. Another method works on the principle that if a pot plant rests on a bed of wet sand the roots will be drawn to the bottom and take in the required amount of water. The water level in the sand is maintained by a lavatory-type cistern joined to the bench with a pipe. The cistern must be sited so that its water level is appropriate for the water level required in the sand.

Trickle irrigation is a way of supplying water directly to the plant or pot at a predetermined rate. A popular form of this is the spaghetti tubing system in which one supply pipe has a large number of individual supply tubes leading off from it. This enables one small pipe to go to each pot and you can then water all the pots in the greenhouse with one turn of the tap.

Hygiene

Although shading is necessary on sunny days, the glass should be kept clean during the winter to admit the maximum amount of light. A long-handled mop will loosen the algae and dirt and a good squirting with a hosepipe will wash it down.

Inside the greenhouse good hygiene is vital. Dead leaves and flowers should be removed frequently. Inspect the plants once or twice a week for signs of pests and disease and, if necessary, use the appropriate spray immediately. Wash down staging and woodwork in autumn and spring.

Smoke cones or pellets are excellent for killing most pests and diseases in a greenhouse. Remember to follow the manufacturer's

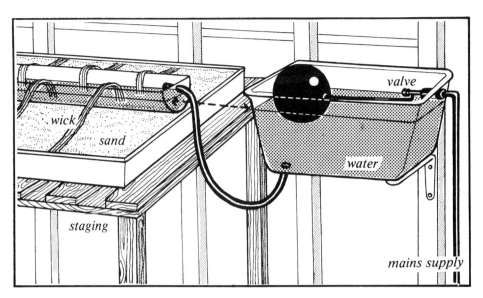

This capillary irrigation system, with a cistern connected to the mains, will keep a sand tray moist indefinitely.

instructions when using them and always light the smoke cone farthest from the door first. If your mobility is limited, clear your exit route in advance.

What are you doing this winter? Are you looking forward to the end of the hectic growing season so that you can get a bit of well-earned rest? There is no reason why you should be stuck for things to do – and this applies even if you have no form of heating whatsoever. The key to getting full use of the greenhouse in winter is advance planning. The later in the year that you start, the more limited your range of options will be.

An unheated greenhouse keeps out extremes of cold, wet and wind, but to be on the safe side don't attempt to over-winter plants which are sensitive to frost – even if you plunge pots in border soil, or cover plants with sacking or polythene, you are taking a risk.

An unheated greenhouse is good for:

● Extending the autumn growing season and getting an early start in spring.
● Getting plants to grow and flower earlier than they would if they spent the winter outside.
● Producing crops of vegetables and herbs for winter consumption.

There are a few things to bear in mind when managing an unheated greenhouse in winter:

● It can actually be colder in the greenhouse than outside on occasions! Watch out for this when the weather is very cold and give the greenhouse some ventilation for a couple of hours around midday. This will allow the cold air (which is heavier than warm air and sinks to ground level) to flow out.
● Plants need less water in winter so don't overdo it. When the weather is very cold keep plants slightly on the dry side.
● Plant roots, even those of hardy plants, are often more prone to suffer from frost than the leaves. So try to insulate them by plunging (burying) small pots in peat or sand and by wrapping larger containers with sacking or straw, for example. You can spread a layer of straw between plants growing in beds to insulate their roots.
● Some pest problems can still be around in winter, like red spider mite and whitefly. The fungus called botrytis can attack seedlings and transplants, especially of lettuce, so you may want to prevent it by spraying with a fungicide, e.g., benomyl, but bear safety in mind.

• Winter is the traditional time for repairs and attending to hygiene. This is going to be more awkward if you have the greenhouse full of plants. You may need to move pots and trays of plants into a shed or indoors while you scrub benches and glass. And you might plan to have a couple of weeks when the greenhouse is clear of crops in border soil.

Making full use of a greenhouse in winter – a month-by-month guide

Here is a month-by-month guide to help you plan for full use of an unheated greenhouse in winter. It is only a guide and doesn't attempt to show the timing of every operation. Months are for northern hemisphere, and may differ for southern hemisphere.

Key: □ In glasshouse   □ Outside   → Start   ⬛ Pot up/sow   🌸 Flower   🌿 Harvest/plant grown

	Jan.	Feb.	Mar.	April	MAY	June	July	Aug.	Sept.	Oct.	Nov.	Dec.
Hardy bulbs	🌸	🌸	🌸							Pot→		🌸
Hardy shrubs	🌸	🌸	🌸								Pot→	
Half hardy shrubs	🌸	🌸	🌸						Pot→			🌸
Hardy Perennials	🌸	🌸	🌸								Pot→	
Hardy Annuals					🌸	🌸				Pot→	Pot	
Hardy Biennials (flower under glass)	🌸	🌸	🌸	Pot→	Pot							
Hardy Biennials (to flower outside)			🌸		🌸		Pot→	Pot	Pot			
Ferns	🌿	🌿	🌿	🌿						Pot	🌿	🌿
Lettuce, e.g. Aug/Sept sown	🌿							Pot→	Pot			🌿
Lettuce sown Nov left under glass			🌿								Pot→	
Lettuce sown Nov to go out March				🌿	🌿						Pot	
Lettuce sown Jan left under glass	Pot→			🌿	🌿							
Mustard and Cress			Pot 🌿							Pot→🌿	Pot 🌿	Pot 🌿
Winter Endive				🌿				Pot→				
Seakale	🌿					Pot→				Pot		🌿
Chicory	Pot 🌿	Pot 🌿	Pot 🌿			Pot→					Pot	Pot 🌿
Radish	Pot→		🌿	🌿								
Hardy herbs	🌿	🌿	🌿								Pot→	🌿
Vegetables (harvest under glass)		Pot→				🌿						
Vegetables (harvest outside)	Pot→						🌿	🌿				
Strawberries				🌿	🌿				Pot→			

─ NINE ─

Indoor seed sowing – making it easier

This does not set out to be 'Everyman's Complete Guide to Seed Sowing', but instead aims to pinpoint the main difficulties that commonly arise in carrying out the task, and to suggest possible ways in which these may be overcome. It almost goes without saying that they are not intended as recommendations, for what suits one person does not necessarily suit another. Rather, they are ideas which we know have proved reliable on many occasions.

Ask about a successful project's origins and often you will be told about the packet or two of seed germinated almost accidentally by a keen gardener, which later transformed a dull paved corner into a dazzling riot of summer colour.

Sadly, however, the other type of seed sowing story is also common – the one that tells of those tiny seeds impossible to sow; the special seeds that fail to germinate; the spindly seedlings that collapse overnight; those which perish during pricking out. It needn't happen either ... If it has happened to you, then ask yourself, what went wrong? Where did the problem lie?

Sometimes, the fault lies with faulty management (viz., the seed tray that dries out over the weekend). A lack of technical knowledge may be responsible – perhaps the seeds were sown too deeply. Alternatively, environmental growing conditions may be inappropriate, with prevailing light, temperature and humidity levels proving quite unsuitable for successful germination and healthy seedling growth. This, incidentally, is a very common problem for indoor gardening projects in centrally heated buildings with low light levels, but rarely an insurmountable one. All these difficulties can usually be rectified with careful planning. Often the problem lies in one of the following areas:

Filling the container with compost

Materials such as the compost, containers and striking-off board need to be placed for maximum accessibility on the work bench. For most people this means an arrangement as in the illustration. Where there is little upper arm strength, the container can be supported in the work surface itself to minimize the lifting movement needed in the transfer of compost. A lightweight plastic scoop, cup or plant pot, of an easy-to-grip shape, can be a great help.

Striking off the compost flush with the top of the seed tray may demand co-ordination skills beyond the ability of some. A simple, narrow board, fitting securely across the width of a standard seed tray, can be slid from one end of the tray to the other to ease this operation.

Firming the compost before sowing

An important factor affecting uniformity of germination is the distribution of air and moisture throughout the compost. Over- or under-compaction of compost, whether throughout the container or locally, encourages irregularity

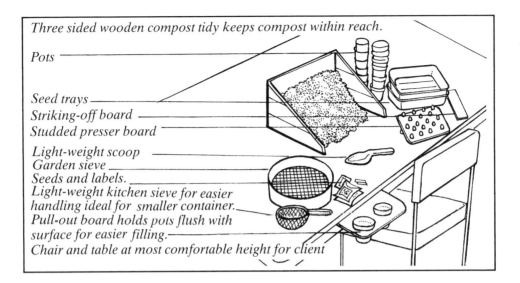

Three sided wooden compost tidy keeps compost within reach.

Pots

Seed trays
Striking-off board
Studded presser board

Light-weight scoop
Garden sieve
Seeds and labels.
Light-weight kitchen sieve for easier
handling ideal for smaller container.
Pull-out board holds pots flush with
surface for easier filling.
Chair and table at most comfortable height for client

of germination. Presser boards the same size as the container are invaluable, but their use requires care, judgement and good motor co-ordination. Correct, even pressure can be applied more easily if a paint mark is made at the correct depth around the inside lip of the container, or, alternatively, if only those containers are used which have a narrow ridge inside the lip onto which the presser board can be pressed.

Sowing the seed – handling

People with limited grip or finger movement may find small seed difficult to pick up and hold. Moistening the fingers may help, as may the use of tweezers or seed sticks. Seed size and shape varies greatly between species, so choose your seed appropriately. Pelleted seed (where small seeds are encased in a clay-like material) is often invaluable, and, if brightly coloured too, helps visually handicapped gardeners considerably. Gardeners with no use of hands may be able to pick up seeds individually by sucking through a pipette or straw and then space sowing.

Sowing the seed – spacing

Even seed distribution is essential for even germination, but in practice the use of the traditional broadcast method may be difficult, even for an able-bodied person. A home-made dispenser, such as a Tic-Tac box, teaspoon or piece of paper may help, as may one of the proprietary hand seed dispensers. But by far the easiest method (given an assurance of seed viability) is to space sow individual seeds at regular, predetermined intervals. There are several ways of doing this. One or two seeds can be sown into shallow depressions on the firmed compost, formed for example by a studded presser board or by the gentle use of a multi-dibber board. A guide can be used, such as a pre-formed grid or wooden spacing board with small holes punched out at regular intervals to the desired spacing, which fits exactly onto the seed tray. One wooden aid, the spacer frame, is particularly useful for blind people, besides being versatile in allowing for several spacing patterns; also coming in handy for the striking of cuttings. Finally, the use of some sort of modular system, where one to four seeds may be sown per individual pot, cell or block, can effectively bypass many spacing difficulties altogether.

Covering the seed

This is normally done by shaking sieved compost over the container until the compost level is flush with the surface. It can be difficult for those with limited mobility or control of movement. Where the expense is justified, a rotary, semi-automatic sieve may be used. This may be on legs, and is operated by turning a handle, the seed tray being placed beneath. In some cases, a small lightweight kitchen sieve may be easier to use than the conventional heavier horticultural models. One can always circumvent the issue by selecting seed that will only germinate in the light, and does not need covering.

Watering the container

The correct use of a watering-can or spray rose for this purpose requires much skill and practice. It is all too easy to compact the compost's surface unduly ('capping'), to saturate it excessively, or to water inadequately or irregularly. All these hinder even germination and subsequent growth. It is far better to adopt the standard practice of standing the container in, say, a shallow cat litter tray of water, removing it once the surface of the compost is damp. Thereafter, standing the container on capillary matting, a damp bed of sand or expanded clay granules is advisable.

Pricking out

In certain circumstances, this activity may be justified, for example, where manual dexterity or hand–eye co-ordination needs improving. However, where concentration spans are limited and accuracy of movement impeded, pricking out is often the task above all others responsible for inducing unnecessary frustration, boredom and damage to seedling stems and root systems! Eliminating it through the use of space sowing or modular systems is generally a good idea both from the gardener's point of view and in the interests of effective plant establishment.

A word about propagators

The electric models are invaluable, particularly where seed sowing or striking cuttings are regular activities. Thermostatically controlled models are the best, but the cheaper unheated

---

Seed spacing frame for visually handicapped people. The spacing bar is located in the notches on either side of the wooden spacing frame which surrounds the seed tray. The small notches along the spacing bar provide an accurate guide for seed spacing. Once a row is complete the bar can be moved to the next row indicated by the appropriate notches.

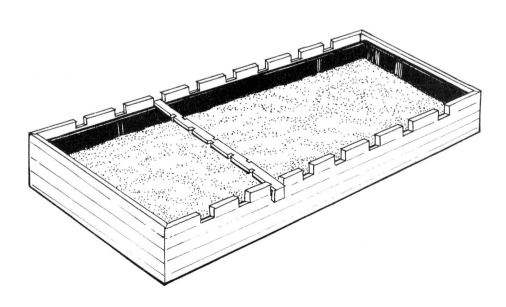

Blind gardener planting out. The photo shows special seed spacing equipment.

propagators are still useful. Choose one with good ventilation control, and site it in a well-lit spot. Finally, don't forget that the more humble seed raiser or seed starter kits are, in effect, mini-propagators and may well be useful too.

Seed sowing – what does it offer the gardener with special needs?

- Enormous range of stimulating plant material to select from to meet individual needs.
- An activity that very nearly everyone can do, given the right approach.
- A cheap means of propagation, particularly if own seed saved and stored in a dessicator for use the following year.
- Either a seasonal or an all-year-round activity in an annual programme.
- Minimal equipment needed, which can range from a sunny windowsill to an electric propagator.
- Potential for use in graded basic education programmes, developing literacy (seed catalogues, labelling), numeracy skills (counting, percentages and growth rates), special concepts.
- Useful in rehabilitation programmes, offering hand–eye co-ordination practice, concentration practice, hand and arm exercise, development of manipulation skills, a sense of expectation and anticipation.
- Wide range of associated activities for programme planning, e.g., choosing seed from garden centres or catalogues (useful winter activity), collection and packaging of own seed, exchange or sale of surplus stocks, seed collages, basic plant biology lessons, seed identification competitions.
- An end product (i.e., the small plant) that can be used in a whole host of different ways to

meet different purposes – plant displays, cooking, craft activities, etc.

- Lots of stimulus, particularly for children (e.g., avocados, peanuts, cress 'animals', sprouting seeds, beans in jars, fruit pips, ferns).

Trees from seeds

Starting is easy. For your collecting you will need polythene bags, ties, labels and a pencil or indelible pen. Those who have difficulty bending may find a 'Garden Grab' or 'Supergrab' good for picking up seeds and berries from the ground. An 'Easikneeler' stool could also help you to reach the ground and pick up the material. One-handed gardeners might find the long-handled flower gatherer an invaluable aid, and the Cut-and-hold secateurs would be ideal for closer work.

Seeds and fruit should always be collected when they are in prime condition, which means that several forays will be necessary over a period of weeks. Remember to label the bags of seeds and fruits using pencil or waterproof ink or you may later confuse similar fruits or varieties of the same species.

Bulky and fleshy seeds and fruits should not be collected in large batches or kept in the containers for too long as they can ferment and heat up, resulting in the embryos of the seeds dying – so store them in small batches, preferably in the refrigerator.

To extract the seeds from large succulent fruits like crab apples and quinces, slice away most of the flesh using a kitchen knife, then squash the core of the fruit through a sieve before leaving in a jar of warm water. After a few days the flesh will float to the surface and can be scooped off. Change the water two or three times to remove all the flesh and the seeds will be found quite clean at the bottom of the jar.

Fruits that are only moderately fleshy like *Berberis* and *Pyracantha* should be squashed then swirled around with water in a shallow bowl. The denser seeds will tend to collect in the centre of the bowl and the debris will float around the bowl perimeter.

Large dry fruits such as capsules can be hand crushed and the seeds sieved from the debris. Fir cones should be placed in a paper bag in the airing cupboard to dry out and then shaken to separate the seeds from the cones. Crumble small seeds or those that have wings by hand so that the viable portion of the seed is not destroyed and can be picked out.

If you do not want to sow the seeds immediately after they have been extracted from the fruits, surface-dry them to prevent fungal rot, and some people choose to dust them with a fungicidal powder. If they are to be used within a couple of days, store them at room temperature in a polythene bag to maintain their moisture content. For long-term storage put the seeds in a labelled polythene bag in the refrigerator. As a general rule, the lower the temperature the more effective the storage will be, as long as the seeds are not frozen.

Before sowing it is necessary to break the dormancy of seeds with hard seed coats. An easy method is to line the inside of a screw-capped jar with coarse sandpaper, put in the seeds, screw down the lid and shake the jar until the seed coats are sufficiently worn down. The damaged seed coat will allow water to be absorbed prior to germination.

Many tree and shrub seeds undergo a period of dormancy which is broken only by exposure to low temperatures. A normally cold winter is sufficient to break this but in order to avoid disappointment it is worth giving your seeds an artificial cold period. This is known as 'stratification'.

To obtain a suitable medium for stratification sieve four volumes (say four kitchen measuring jugs) of coarse moss peat into a large plastic bowl. Add one volume of water to make this damp, and one volume of seeds. Put in one more volume of coarse grit in order to improve aeration. Place the mixture in a polythene bag and label, allowing two or three days for water absorption before putting the bag into the refrigerator (not deep freeze). Turn and shake the bag every week to encourage circulation of air around the seeds. The cold period required varies according to species.

But how about growing the seeds? An open ground seedbed is best, and it can be planned in rows, squares or in the form of raised beds for those who work from a wheelchair. Even a very small area of ground can be used as seedlings are intensively grown. As the root systems of many trees and shrubs live in symbiosis (in mutual benefit) with some types of microscopic fungus, ensure their presence by collecting a little leaf mould from around the trees harvested, and work this into your seedbed.

The preparation of the seedbed should be thorough and good drainage is essential. The use of raised beds ensures this and indeed many foresters construct boarded-in seedbeds about 35–45 cm. (15–18 in.) high for this reason.

Although seedlings are grown intensively, make sure that they do not grow too thickly. Space out large seeds by hand while smaller ones can be lightly hand broadcast. Once they are sown, firm the seeds into the seedbed using a presser board or the back of a spade. Then cover them with grit to a depth of about 1 cm. ($\frac{1}{2}$ in.).

This will ensure good surface drainage and absorb the impact of raindrops. Remember to label your seedbeds clearly in waterproof ink.

Tree and shrub seedlings in the wild are protected from the wind and frost by the woodland or scrub canopy. Protection is easily provided by laying pea sticks over the seedbed. Any weed seedlings that do appear can be pulled out while the roots are still in the grit rather than in the soil.

Within a short period of time your seedbed will be a miniature forest. Have fun caring for the seedlings and then plan carefully how you will enhance your local landscape for generations yet to come. However, remember that due to cross-pollination your seedlings may not grow to be exactly like their parents, so if you sell the plants ensure the customer isn't misled into thinking he is getting a 'pure strain'.

TEN

Hardwood cuttings

'Nothing succeeds like success'. Yet gardening is a medium in which it is only too apparent when there is a failure. It is difficult to be enthusiastic over half a dozen trays of rotting seedlings or cuttings, so it is good to tackle a gardening task at which success is almost guaranteed. The propagation of shrubs from hardwood cuttings is such an activity, and as an added bonus the work takes place during the less hectic periods of the gardening year.

Why is this method so easy?

A hardwood cutting is made during the dormant season from a fully mature stem of a deciduous tree or shrub. Because the wood is ripe and because there are no leaves on the cutting very little environmental control is necessary for successful rooting. The cuttings can be taken at any time between leaf-fall in autumn and bud-break in the spring although, in practice, the autumn is the best time. No special equipment is necessary, assuming that you have a pair of secateurs and a spade, and there is no need for a greenhouse or frame. One-handed gardeners will find cut-and-hold type secateurs useful.

How to take a cutting

Remove a hardwood stem from the shrub using secateurs. Always choose material that has grown during the current year and, if taking off a side shoot, cut flush with the parent stem to avoid leaving unsightly stumps and snags. Make a sloping cut immediately above the bud that you chose as your top one, and a horizontal cut 15 cm. (6 in.) below it, regardless of the position of any lower buds. Although this cutting should root easily, some people like to dip the lower cut surface in hormone rooting powder, shaking off any surplus that sticks to the wood.

Treatment of cuttings

Hardwood cuttings can simply be planted into well-cultivated soil as soon as they have been taken. If you take cuttings during the autumn, though, it is often better to tie up ten or twelve in a bundle and bury them in sand with just the top inch showing. This can be in a box or flowerpot, or just in sandy soil outside. There is no need to water them unless the sand gets really dry.

When the dormant buds are just starting to swell in the early spring, thoroughly prepare a planting-out bed by digging it deeply and preparing a tilth. Take the by now callussed-over cuttings from the bundles in the sand and place them vertically into a slit or furrow in the soil 10 cm. (5 in.) deep and 30 cm. (12 in.) apart. Firm the soil, leaving about 2.5 cm. (1 in.) of each cutting exposed. By the autumn the cuttings will have rooted and can be transplanted to their final situations in the garden.

*   *   *

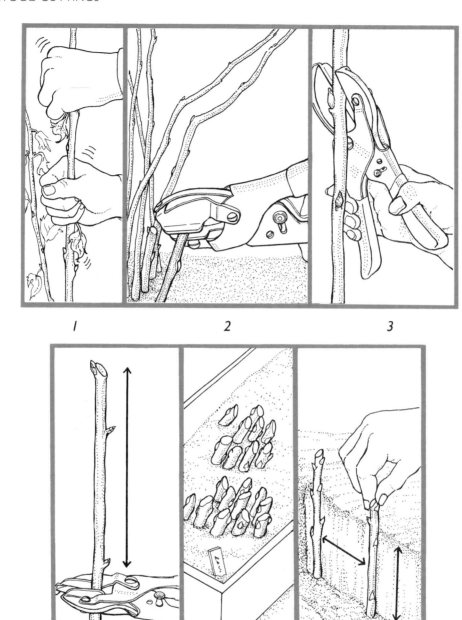

1. In the early autumn, run a hand down a leafy stem on the parent plant and if the leaves fall off, the time is right to take cuttings.

2. Remove a hardwood stem with its current year's growth. Gardeners with only one hand will find cut-and-hold secateurs helpful for this job.

3. Make a sloping cut just above the proposed bud.

4. Make a horizontal cut 15 cm. (6 in.) below your top cut and then dip the lower cut into hormone rooting powder.

5. Place bundles of cuttings in a sand-box leaving the top 2.5 cm. (1 in.) showing.

6. Before bud-break dig the planting-out bed thoroughly and make a furrow 12 cm. (5 in.) deep. Plant the cuttings 30 cm. (12 in.) apart in the furrow.

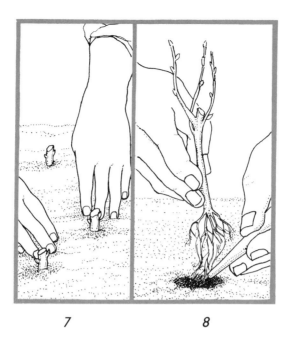

7

8

7. Firm back the soil leaving 2.5 cm. (1 in.) of the cutting exposed.
8. In the following autumn lift the rooted cuttings for transplanting.

Bush or standard?

To grow a plant with only one stem, such as a tree or standard, encourage only the top bud to develop on the cutting. This can be done by removing the lower buds with your thumb or with a knife before bundling up the cuttings and inserting them into the sand.

The same effect can also be achieved by burying the cuttings more deeply, so that each one is covered by about 1 cm. ($\frac{1}{2}$ in.) of soil. Usually only the top bud develops.

A special case – pithy plants

Some shrubs, such as *Forsythia* or *Kerria*, have a very soft pith which tends to go rotten, killing the cuttings. There are two ways of overcoming the problem. Firstly, make the cutting 15 cm. (6 in.) long and seal the hollow, pithy stem at the top and bottom with candle wax or Arbrex.

Alternatively, make the basal cut at a node (or bud) because the stem will be solid at that point and infection cannot gain entry. Although you should try to keep to about 15 cm. (6 in.), this method will give rise to cuttings of different lengths, but they will certainly grow just as well.

Plants that can be successfully propagated from hardwood cuttings

Aucuba, blackcurrant, box, *Cornus* (dogwood), *Cotoneaster* (large shrub varieties), *Deutzia*, Escallonia, *Forsythia*, gooseberry, honeysuckle, jasmine, *Kerria* (bachelor's buttonholes), *Laburnum*, mulberry, *Philadelphus* (mock orange), poplar, potentilla, privet, *Ribes* (flowering currant), roses, *Salix* (willow), *Sambucus* (elder), *Spiraea*, *Symphoricarpus* (snowberry), *Viburnum* (deciduous types), Weigela.

Soft wood cuttings. Take these in late spring or early summer. Ideal for many aromatic shrubby herbs.

- Select vigorous new shoots, 7–10 cm. (about 3–4 in.) long, without flower buds. Pull away from the main woody stem including a small heel of wood.
- Strip off lower leaves and insert around the edge of a flowerpot containing a 50/50 mix of peat and sand.
- Covering with a plastic bag often seems to help, but this should be removed regularly for ventilation, and the pot placed in light shade.

Semi-ripe cuttings. These are taken and treated in the same way, but from longer shoots in early autumn. Suitable for rosemary, lemon verbena, bay, myrtle and many others.

Layering. This happens naturally when stems touch the soil and form roots. Many plants have this capacity. It can be stimulated artificially by pegging the stem down into surrounding soil. Early to late summer is the ideal time; new roots form rapidly. Herbs that can be propagated in this way are: thymes, marjorams, calamint, winter savory, hyssop.

Handy ideas

ELEVEN

Handy hints

Adaptations and gadgets for easier gardening: do you feel bombarded with information encouraging you to buy all manner of expensive tools and gadgets?

Here are some handy hints to save you money and to make your gardening easier.

Why not look around your house, garage or shed and see if you can use or adapt some items to make gardening easier? For example, an old kitchen knife is very useful for teasing out those awkward weeds that always seem to come up in the cracks and spaces in paving. If the handle is not comfortable, bind it with sponge and cloth.

A small builder's trowel is comfortable to use for weeding and often does the job better than a trowel or hand-fork.

An old kitchen sieve can be used to sieve small amounts of compost for covering seeds in trays or pots. On the other hand, if attached to a stout cane or old broom handle, the sieve (or a colander) can be used to pick fruit that is out of reach – provided the fruit is fairly ripe and ready to drop. The same gadget is useful for picking up potatoes that have been dug and are lying on the surface – for those who can't bend or who are wheelchair-bound.

*　　*　　*

Putting down a line and sowing large seeds without bending

If you can't reach the ground there is an easy method of laying a garden line to get a straight drill and for sowing large seeds. All you need for the line is two stout dowels or broom handles, a fishing reel and a length of string to suit the length of the drill. Simply attach the string to one of the poles, pass it through a hook on the second pole and then up to a fishing reel fixed near the top of this pole. You can then push one pole into the soil at each side of the plot where you want to make the drill and tighten the line with the reel. Using the line for guidance, make a straight drill using a long-handled hoe.

To sow your seeds without bending or from a sitting position, simply place one end of a length of plastic piping where you want your first seed in the drill and then drop the seed down the pipe. Move the pipe along the drill to sow the next seed; spacing will depend on the size of plant, so check the seed packet for the correct distance. Practice will show you how small a seed will easily drop down the pipe.

Keep those hanging baskets well watered!

To make the most of a display in a hanging basket you must make sure that it does not dry out. If you do not have a lance-spray attachment to

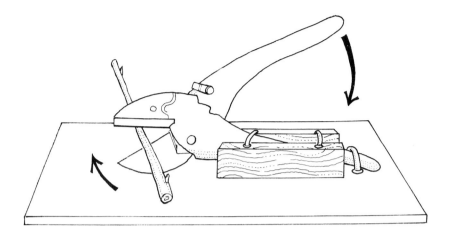

your hosepipe, this could mean that you have to get the hanging basket down from its hook daily or even twice daily. If you can't water the basket in place, why not put it on a pulley? You can then simply lower it to a convenient height for watering and hoist it again when the surplus water has drained off. A well-watered hanging basket is very heavy. Make sure you use a strong nylon rope, that all the fittings are secure and that the rope is always firmly anchored to the wall fitting.

Mini-greenhouses

Many vegetables are now packed for sale in plastic containers. These include beansprouts, tomatoes, mushrooms and some of the tropical fruits. These containers are ideal for using as mini-greenhouses. The green or opaque contain-

ers can be used as bases while the clear plastic ones are ideal as tops. All you need to do is make sure that the base and the top are the same size and that there are adequate drainage holes in the base. Fill the base with compost, put in the cuttings or seed and put the top on. This will provide a high-humidity environment that will suit cuttings and the germination of many seeds. Take care not to place your mini-greenhouse in direct sunlight or the effect will be to create an oven!

Making holes in the bases of plastic containers can sometimes be quite difficult, particularly with those of thicker plastic. One solution to this problem is to use an old soldering iron. This will easily burn the holes through. BE SURE TO DO THIS IN A WELL-VENTILATED ROOM AS THE FUMES GIVEN OFF FROM BURNING PLASTIC ARE POISONOUS.

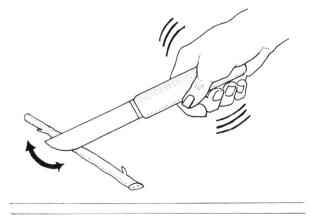

Taking cuttings is difficult to manage if you only have the use of one hand, so these tips may help to overcome the problems:

Fix a pair of secateurs to a board as opposite. Once you have gathered plant material you can trim it to the required length for cuttings by placing it between the blades of the secateurs and cutting by pressing down on the free handle.

Alternatively, a knife with a curved blade will cut through softer plant material if you use an easy rocking motion (see opposite).

Once cuttings have rooted, they will need to be potted up. The rooted cutting can be held in position in the pot by pegging a couple of clothes pegs to the stem and then balancing the ends of the pegs on the pot rim. The cutting is held in place by the pegs while the compost is filled in round it.

Potting on

This term describes moving plants on from one pot to another larger one. Plants look best if they are in the centre of the pot. A method to make sure of this centring is to work as follows:

1. Cut a circular cardboard template that will neatly rest in the top of the larger pot.
2. Cut a slit in the template as shown.
3. Put enough compost into the larger pot to ensure that when the smaller pot is placed inside, both pot rims are level.
4. Knock the plant out of the smaller pot and position it in the centre of the template as shown.
5. Place the plant and template in the larger pot, resting the template on the inner ridge.
6. Carefully remove the template and fill in compost around the centred plant.

Cheap plant labels

A good gardener will make sure that everything in the greenhouse is well labelled. White plastic labels are most frequently used and are available at all garden centres. Plant names should be written on them in pencil as this will not wash off. Labels can be scraped clean to be used again. If you want to save money on labels, cut up a used

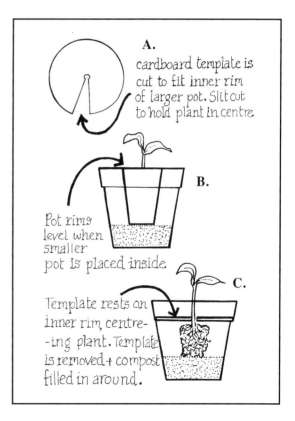

A. cardboard template is cut to fit inner rim of larger pot. Slit cut to hold plant in centre

B. Pot rims level when smaller pot is placed inside

C. Template rests on inner rim, centre-ing plant. Template is removed + compost filled in around.

plastic washing-up liquid bottle (vertically) into label-sized strips.

A home-made 'spiker' — for a healthy lawn

Constant mowing and walking over a lawn will gradually compact it, squeezing the air out of the soil, and making it difficult for water to drain through. If this is combined with a large amount of 'thatch' (the accumulation of dead or fibrous material on the soil surface) it will lead to poor penetration of water and fertilizers, resulting in unsatisfactory root development and therefore poor grass growth. In other words – an unhealthy lawn!

To overcome these problems, the lawn needs aerating. For this the lawn needs to be 'spiked' to a depth of about 7.5 cm. (3 in.). Holes should be spiked at intervals of 10–15 cm. (4–6 in.). There are a number of spikers available on the market, or a garden fork could be used.

Here is a way of making a spiker at home. It is particularly useful if you cannot bend, or only have the use of one hand. As the diagram shows, it is made by driving 10 cm. (4 in.) nails into a 2 cm. ($\frac{3}{4}$ in.) thick board at intervals of 10–15 cm. (4–6 in.). A thin metal sheet is placed on top of the nail heads and then 'sandwiched' beneath another board the same size. The spiker 'sandwich' can be held together using four bolts. The rope handle is then attached at each end of the board with staple nails. Choose a comfortable length of rope so that you don't have to bend when using the spiker.

To operate, simply place your foot on the board and tread on it so that the spikes sink into the lawn. Lift it to the next position using the rope and repeat the operation until the whole lawn area has been spiked.

Aerating is best done in the spring and you should soon notice an improvement in your lawn.

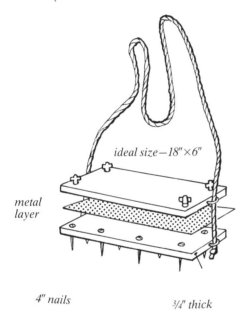

ideal size—18"×6"

metal layer

4" nails

¾" thick

TWELVE

Have you got that 'sink-ing' feeling?

Why not make a sink garden?

This can provide a delightful micro-landscape which offers an ideal setting for all kinds of dwarf and diminutive plant beauties often lost in an ordinary garden environment.

The stone sinks of old are now very rare but a keen eye can often spot discarded porcelain items on skips – kitchen sinks, lavatory pans or washbasins can all be adapted in a similar way.

To make the sink look more authentic or, in other words, less like an old discarded sink, a coating of cement and peat mixture can be applied to the outside – this substance is known as hyper-tufa. It looks very natural, closely resembling the real tufa, a stone found only in a few areas, which is light in weight and very porous, being composed of deposits rich in lime laid down by rivers. Naturally this lime-based medium would restrict the choice of plants, but hyper-tufa is not so alkaline. The choice of soil used in the finished container will be all that determines your choice of plants.

The resulting old-stone effect of the container will ensure that the plants become the focus of attention in a tasteful setting.

How to do it

You will need help as the sinks are extremely heavy

All pipe fittings should be removed and the sink must be thoroughly cleaned with detergent and rinsed well. Select its position carefully as once the sink is mounted it will be well-nigh impossible to manœuvre.

Drainage will be critical, so the sink needs to be positioned above ground level. Choose a suitable height to meet individual needs. All-round access by wheelchair may well be a consideration and best working height needs to be decided upon. As regards aspect, an open, airy and, perhaps, west-facing location is ideal.

The sink can balance on a central plinth or on supports at each end. Brick, stone, breeze-blocks, old chimney stacks, an already existing raised bed or wall may all be suitable. The main requirement is that the garden is safe and firmly supported.

The sink can now be transformed *in situ*. Cool, not frosty, weather is ideal for carrying out this work.

What you will need

1. The sink (*in situ*).
2. Some plastic to put underneath to catch drips.
3. Medium-size tin of all-purpose contact adhesive, e.g., Unibond, and spreader (old paintbrush or piece of wood).
4. Rubber gloves which can afterwards be discarded.
5. A 2-gallon bucket (or 2 × 1 gall.).

6. A 'small' bag of ready-mix cement (enough to fill half the bucket).
7. Sphagnum moss peat (enough to fill the other half).
8. Water for mixing and stick or spade for mixing with.
9. Crocks to go over the plug-hole.
10. 5 cm. (2 in.) stones or grit for drainage.
11. Soil mix to go in the container.
12. Plants of your choice (see list on page 79).
13. Some rocks if desired to landscape the sink garden.
14. Grit to cover exposed soil.

What to do

1. Soak half a bucket of peat in water.
2. Paint the outside of the sink and 10 cm. (4 in.) down the inside with a coating of the contact adhesive. Be generous or else the hyper-tufa will not stay on, leaving bald patches showing. Use an old paintbrush or a spreader, whichever seems easiest. This is a voyage of discovery.
3. Allow this to dry for about $1\frac{1}{2}$ hours, *then* mix up some hyper-tufa.
4. Using equal parts of soaked peat and ready-mix cement, fill half your bucket (it is best to mix a little at a time).
5. THE AMOUNT OF WATER YOU ADD IS CRITICAL. Add water VERY CAREFULLY (from a watering-can or milk bottle), stirring the mess with a stick in the bucket. If this seems hard, empty it out on plastic and try mixing with a trowel.
6. When this mixture has the consistency of stiff porridge it is ready. YOU DON'T NEED MUCH WATER. TOO MUCH WATER IS A DISASTER AS IT WILL MAKE THE MIX TOO WET.
7. What you have now is half a bucket of hyper-tufa.
8. Apply more adhesive to a small section of the sink, say half of one side.
9. Leave it for a short while until it is tacky, then slap the mixture on about 1 cm. ($\frac{1}{2}$ in.) thick. This is a wonderfully messy job. Do it with your hands (rubber gloves needed) or use a builder's trowel. It needs to be pressed

firmly onto the adhesive but, of course, bits will keep falling off. If a small part is attempted at a time, panic will be kept to a minimum!

10. Carry on in this mode until you have used up the first mix, then start again from point **4**.

11. When the sink is covered (a 2-gallon bucket-ful of the mix is usually enough for a normal-size sink), cover it with plastic and allow it to dry. The longer it takes to set the stronger it will become, so a sprinkle of water after a day or so will not come amiss.

12. The coating can be left with a rough but ready appearance, or marked in lines or brushed smooth to please individual tastes. It is better to make marks when the mixture hardens.

13. When 24 hours have elapsed, brush a little sour milk or organic liquid fertilizer onto the surface. This will encourage the growth of mosses and lichens to increase the natural appearance.

14. Leave this for at least two weeks before attempting to fill the container with soil, or plant it up.

Drainage

DRAINAGE is crucial, but should present no problem because of the plug-hole. Cover this with crocks – slates, tiles or perforated zinc – to prevent it being blocked up. Add at least 5 cm. (2 in.) of stones, rubble or gravel, then a layer of sphagnum peat if you have any left, then soil (see diagram on page 79).

Soil

A gritty mix is to be recommended, perhaps John Innes No. 1 or 2 with extra grit if possible, or good garden soil mixed with some John Innes No. 1 or 2 and sharp sand. Small rocks can be arranged on top to give an added dimension and to provide extra drainage for certain plants. Soak the soil and allow it to settle for a few days.

A weak solution of permanganate of potash sprinkled over the whole sink at this point will prevent woodlice or slugs from becoming too aggressive.

After planting, chippings or shingle can be placed on any exposed soil, to keep plants clean, deter weed seedlings, conserve moisture and give an overall neat appearance to this tiny garden.

Planting

SOME HINTS: If you desire a miniature rock garden plant a few dwarf conifers, perhaps two or three of different shapes and colours; pointed or bushy, green, golden or blue. Among any protruding rocks add tiny rosette- and cushion-forming plants which will never become rampant. It is best not to overcrowd with plants at first as this will lead to losses, so be prepared to admire more rock chippings than plants until the garden is established.

You could choose a single plant family with infinite variety to fill the whole sink on their own, e.g., succulents such as *Sedum* (stonecrop), *Sempervivum* (houseleeks) or rosette-type plants like *Saxifraga* (rock-foil).

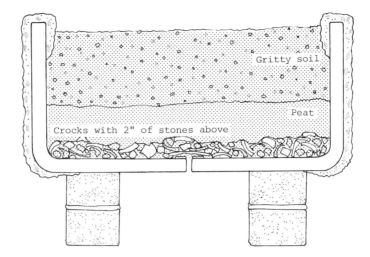

Tiny mosses, hardy ferns or miniature bulbs will add extra interest.

Alternatively, the sink can be used for seasonal display, e.g., dwarf bulbs of unusual type for winter and spring which can be lifted when foliage begins to die down and preserved for the next year. Likewise annuals, dwarf shrubs, miniature roses or evergreen trailers can be included for summer and autumn display.

Plants for sink gardens – some ideas

Conifers: These grow only about 1 cm. ($\frac{1}{2}$ in.) or so per year. *Chamaecyparis obtusa* 'Nana Gracilis': pyramid shape; *Juniperus communis* 'Compressa': columnar, blue-green; *Picea abies* 'Little Gem': bright green dome; *Cryptomeria japonica* 'Compressa': bronze foliage in winter.

Dwarf shrubs: *Andromeda polifolia* 'Compacta': 'needs peaty soil' 20 cm. (8 in.) spread, evergreen, pink or white bell-like flowers in early summer; *Genista delphinensis*: large yellow flowers on tightly congested mats, 10 cm. (4 in.) spread; *Daphne arbuscula*: slow-growing, 15 cm. (6 in.), rosy pink waxy flowers.

Cushion-forming plants: *Armeria juniperifolia* 'Bevans Variety': pink flowers; *Dionysia aretioides*: bright yellow flowers in spring; *Gentiana acaulis*: violet-blue, spring to summer; *Saxifraga grisebachii*: curious mauve-red flowers on long stems in spring with silver foliage.

Aftercare

Watering on first planting is important. Until plants are established they need to be watered thoroughly in dry weather – a rose on the watering-can is necessary to give a gentle spray.
Feeding: bone-meal for alpine and shrubby plants, liquid fertilizer during the growing season for annuals.

Maintenance

Dead-heading needs attention and weed removal also. Plants that try and outgrow their allotted space need to be dealt with firmly.

Soil will need renewing only if annual plants are grown – the top 10 cm. (4 in.) or so will suffice. A close and loving eye will spot any disease early and prompt attention will bring its rewards.

largest plant

hole diameter

medium plant

trailers

Rooting cuttings — smallest size bottle for cuttings, largest for specimen fern.

The hanging or standing bottle garden — stand or hang in good light, not bright sunlight. Water after planting.

THIRTEEN

Don't throw it away – grow something in it!

Fizzy lemonade, cola or spring water are often sold in sturdy polythene 'tubes' of varying sizes and colours. Why throw them away when they can help with your growing? They cost nothing, yet add a different dimension to the world of gardening. Landscape your bottle, hang it up, give it away as a present! Here are some ideas – and you can develop more of your own.

The hanging or standing garden

A hole is made in the centre of the bottle, approx. 10 cm. (4 in.) diameter, 5 cm. (2 in.) from the base. It should be large enough to insert compost and plants. Allow 3–5 cm. (1½–2 in.) at the bottom of the bottle to hold the compost. Drainage problems are overcome by either piercing a few holes in the bottom, or placing gravel and charcoal underneath the compost. The clear plastic makes the most of available light and helps to keep up humidity levels to aid growth of the selected plant material. Some extremely attractive foliage plants are available; small rooted cuttings which are known as 'tots' in the nursery trade. Try putting medium-sized plants at the rear and trailing ones at the edge of the hole.

Suitable plants

Pilea species – the aluminium plant, varieties *P.* 'Bronze' or *P.* 'Moon Valley'.

Peperomia – a dwarf variety called 'Pixie' is available, or *P. caperata*.
Hypoestes – the polka dot plant.
Fittonia – with white or pink leaf veins.
Plantlets of *Chlorophytum* (spider plant), or *Saxifraga stolonifera* (mother of thousands) may be used; a single plant of the latter could occupy the entire bottle, with subsequent plantlets hanging out of the mouth.
Tradescantias (wandering sailor) of various colours or patterned ivies may be planted so that they cascade attractively from the hole.
Plectranthus (swedish ivy).
Ficus pumila (creeping fig).
Rhoicissus (grape ivy).
The last three plants are suitable subjects for trailing.

Rooting cuttings – stem or leaf

Cut a three-sided flap in the bottle that can be opened like a door, leaving 5 cm. (2 in.) at the bottom of the bottle for the compost. Insert media and cuttings through the door, then close the door to create an extremely moist and warm environment ideal for rooting. The bottle should be kept in a good light (but not direct sunlight) and no watering is needed. This method is also ideal for slow-growing plants that need extremely moist conditions, e.g. *Pteris cretica* (ribbon fern).

*   *   *

Suitable plants

Cuttings of *Pilea cadierei* (aluminium plant), a native of Vietnam, root in two or three weeks.
Iresine herbstii (beefsteak plant).
Euonymus; dwarf varieties.
Impatiens (Busy Lizzie).
Saintpaulia (African violet).

Two or three cuttings of *Tradescantia* inserted in the bottle and pinched out frequently would, in a very short time, fill the container and push their way out through the flap.

Propagation

The base of the bottle may be removed; it is usually stuck on with strong glue so soak it in warm water first. Use these shallow containers for sowing or chitting seeds in; they have small drainage holes. Once the bottom is removed a round clear base is revealed on the bottle. Cut a long flap, three-sided, practically the whole length of the bottle and approximately 5 cm. (2 in.) wide. Secure the flap back with an elastic band or string, which allows a free area to work in. The bottle, laid on its side, may be half filled with a suitable medium – a gritty seed compost, vermiculite for sowing seeds or granules such as Hortag or Leca, which, when topped up with water, can be used for rooting cuttings hydroponically. The former method is ideal for germinating seeds as, when the lid is closed back, the bottle is completely closed creating a miniature greenhouse. Many varieties of half-hardy annuals can be started in this way, also vegetables and tomatoes. As soon as the seeds germinate, ventilation is needed (see diagram on page 84).

Use this method, too, to start off exotic seeds and pips, such as mango, date, lychee, as well as orange, lemon or pomegranate. Place these in a dark and warm place after sowing and check every week for signs of germination.

Herb tower

Remove the label from a large bottle (the coloured ones may also be used for this) and, with a sharp knife, make holes about 5 cm. (2 in.) diameter all the way round the bottle, leaving about 2.5 cm. (1 in.) between them – on a large bottle seven or eight holes can be made. Through the top of the bottle insert a piece of thin plastic or metal pipe, with holes pierced all the way along, until it reaches the bottom of the bottle. Push compost (perhaps a loam-based compost such as John Innes No. 1 would be best) through all the holes to fill the bottle completely. If the compost is moist it will stay in place. Using parsley or thyme seedlings, or breaking up established plants, place small sections of plant material in the holes, gently firming in. Water through the top of the bottle down the pipe. Place on a light kitchen windowsill. This little contraption allows fresh herbs to be enjoyed all the year round. Try growing a different herb in each hole! Also, this idea could be used to grow indoor trailing plants (a cutting in each hole) or the Indian strawberry plant (*Duchesnea*).

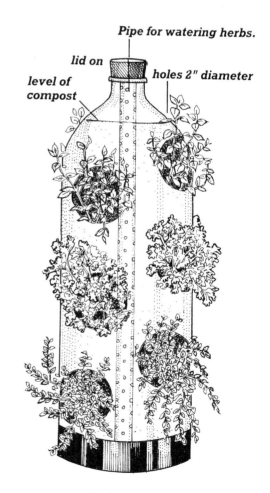

Pipe for watering herbs.

lid on

level of compost

holes 2" diameter

Herb tower.

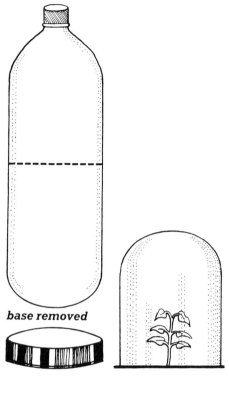

base removed

Cloche.

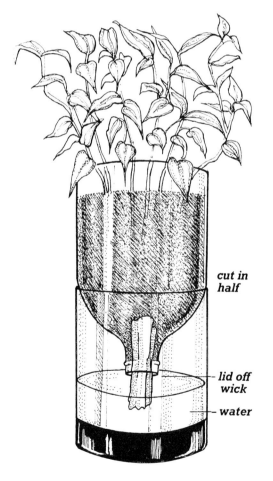

cut in
half

lid off
wick

water

Self-watering plant pot.

Cloche

Perhaps the most obvious use: the largest size clear bottle, with the base removed, can be cut in half horizontally to make a perfect cloche for delicate seedlings and young plants. Bottles used in this way do become very brittle and start curling up after a while. This is the effect of ultra-violet light, but they are effective for those vital few weeks when late frosts may still lurk.

Self-watering plant pot

The bottle, clear or coloured, is cut in half horizontally (keeping the base attached). Fill the bottom half with water. The top half is inverted and some absorbent material pushed through the pouring hole. Then it is planted and placed so that it fits into the lower half of the bottle and the wick, immersed in the water, becomes self-sufficient for up to two weeks, depending on plant type, temperature and light.

Conclusion

These days, when nearly everything one buys in a supermarket or take-away food shop comes in a strong plastic or polystyrene container, it is less necessary to buy special seed trays and pots, as the scope for recycling is endless. Whatever else you do, don't throw containers away, and do enjoy your gardening!

Propagator.

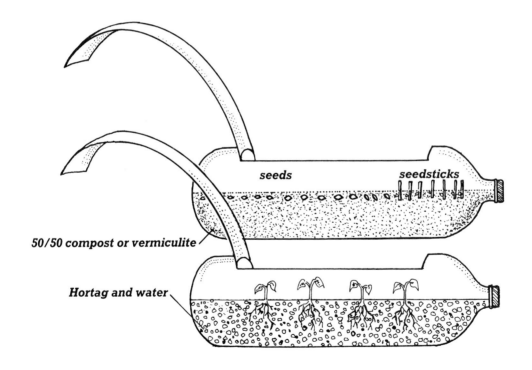

seeds   seedsticks

50/50 compost or vermiculite

Hortag and water

──FOURTEEN──

Nylon building blocks and grow bags

Adapting your garden to suit your abilities can be expensive. Even if you can afford it, finding the right builder and getting the job done is sometimes exhausting, messy and just too much to cope with. Here is a method discovered by John Ward, a former Superintending Architect, which can save you money and trouble – and give you fun into the bargain.

Some years ago, when considering possible forms of cheap homes for refugees living in the shanty towns of the great cities of the world, he wondered why sandbags were not more widely used. Jute bags were expensive and rotted, so what was needed was some form of nylon bag – especially if it was being thrown away.

He experimented with laddered and discarded nylon tights – and the result was that he found earth-filled tights extremely versatile to use, and that they weathered quickly to look like stones.

How to make them

Firstly, one leg of a pair of tights has to be put into the other, ensuring the toes are completely together. This forms a double-layer stocking. A bucket is then filled with compost. In order to get this into the tights, feed them onto the pipe-end of a standard PVC rainwater hopper, fixing the waistband of the tights to the top of the hopper by means of two bulldog paper clips. Then, supporting the tights around the bottom of the hopper, pour the compost from the bucket, allowing it to drop right into the toe of the tights.

When all the compost has dropped through, take the tights off the hopper and hit them on the ground, forming then into a round ball-like shape. Tie the tights in a knot just above the compost, and then double the tights back over the bag, turning them inside out. When you have turned the whole thing upside down tie another knot. This now gives four thicknesses of nylon around the compost. Repeat the process using the waist section of the tights the final time. This finally gives five thicknesses of nylon to the bag, which is now remarkably strong and can be beaten into any shape, and is suitable for bonding in with other bags. To make the whole thing tidier cut off any spare nylon.

These bags are now very suitable for building up table-height planters or walls. Because of the ease of handling, walls or boxes can be made of any shape. A further advantage is that the nylon is soft to the touch and therefore does not damage the skin of anyone who scuffs against the wall.

Not only can the bags be used for walling but also as growbags in which seed, bulbs or plants can be planted, provided that suitable growing material is put in the bags. When they have been shaped for incorporation in the wall, holes are cut with a knife or screwdriver, and then enlarged to take the planting material. Of course the range of plants that can be used is considerable, giving a wide spectrum of colour, texture, shape, fragrance and blossom. As each bag is an

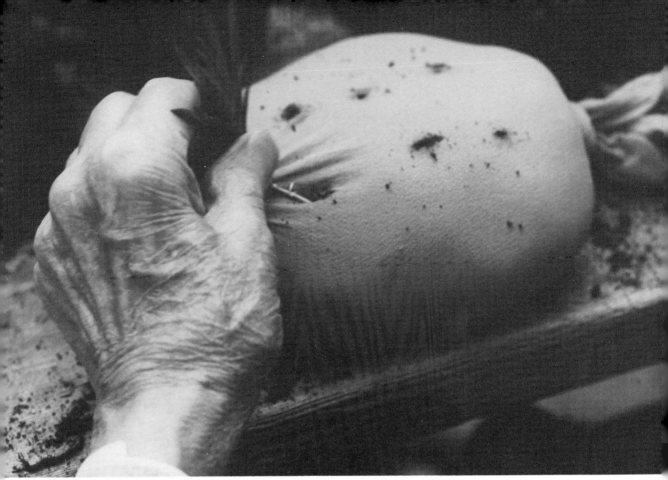

A growbag made from nylon tights.

entity, the growing material in the bag can be designed to support the plant selected. It also gives considerable flexibility in placing the bags in relation to each other, and also in rearranging them with the change of the seasons.

Another advantage of using such bags is that the planting comes right to the edge, so that the gardener does not have to reach across a brick or concrete ledge.

Bags of this sort can easily be worked on by a person in a wheelchair by using a tray on one's lap. The bag can then be placed outside at a height where it can be seen by those inside. Bags can also be kept indoors by placing them in waterproof trays. The nylon seems to have the quality of drawing water up the sides of the bag and irrigating the plants. This may well prove to be an advantage where propagation is intended, as the bags could sit directly on the water-absorbent material used on benches for propagation.

Where there is any possibility that the sides of a planting box or raised flower bed may bulge, alternate courses of bags can be tied together thus providing an element of reinforcement. Walls or boxes of this sort can form raised planters on any hard paving. Seating can be formed, either in walling or supporting a timber bench.

In order to provide a working bench for someone in a wheelchair it is possible to tie thin wooden stakes together with old nylons, and then anchor them down on top of a planting box made from nylon building blocks.

A further area in which these bags can be used is that of the water garden. They can form very effective edges to a pond, covering and protecting the liner. Grass grows very effectively through the nylon so that it can form the edge of a lawn coming right down to the water. They can also be used for aquatic plants needing varying depths of water. This facilitates the moving of plants round the edge of a pond.

Nylon bags can form the walls of a raised pond, thus enabling people with a disability to get near water and enjoy aquatic plants round the edge.

These are only some of the uses to which such bags can be put. No doubt the fertile minds of gardeners could extend the range.

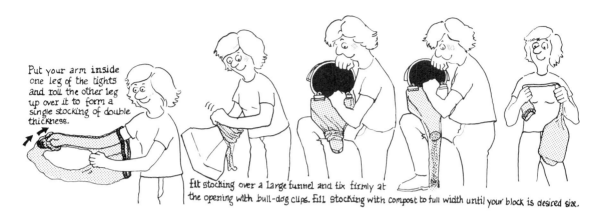

Put your arm inside one leg of the tights and roll the other leg up over it to form a single stocking of double thickness.

Fit stocking over a large funnel and fix firmly at the opening with bull-dog clips. Fill stocking with compost to full width until your block is desired size.

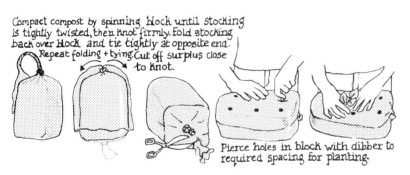

Compact compost by spinning block until stocking is tightly twisted, then knot firmly. Fold stocking back over block and tie tightly at opposite end. Repeat folding + tying. Cut off surplus close to knot.

Pierce holes in block with dibber to required spacing for planting.

How to make your nylon building blocks.

FIFTEEN

Herbs in the home and garden

From pan scrubbers to slug repellents, hair oils to aphid cures, salads to pomanders . . . it seems there is no end to the number of ways in which herbs can be put to good use.

Herbs give value for money without demanding much in return, and most gardeners get involved with them in some way – one can hardly avoid getting involved with a chive plant that suddenly sends out beautiful onion-flavoured flowers, or a lemon verbena that, when accidentally brushed against, evokes memories of sherbet and childhood.

So if you want to make your home colourful, cleaner, pest-free, fragrant, decorative and much more, read on.

Historically, herbs have not only been consumed to purify the body, but also applied in various ways – to mask odours, nourish, cleanse, and colour the skin and hair. Certain herbs have properties thought to promote cell growth and healing, acting as antiseptics or supplying minerals, vitamins and oils. Herbal cosmetics are often a safe alternative for people who experience allergic reactions to commercial preparations.

Bath infusions

A healthy way to refresh yourself. Do not put herbs straight into the bath, but use a strong infusion, or put crushed herbs into a muslin bag and hang from the tap as the water is running. To soften the water add a handful of fine oatmeal.

Rosemary is a great favourite; **marjoram** is reputed to relieve stiffness; **camomile flowers** will calm you. Try **balm, mint** of all kinds, **comfrey, nettles**. (You will not get stung!)

Aromatherapy

Our sense of smell is one of our most compelling senses and, of all the aspects of herbs, their aromatic qualities are often the most immediately apparent. Simply brushing past many herbs is sufficient to release concentrations of scent; these aromatic substances are essential oils or volatile oils. Many can be extracted by distillation from the fresh plant, and are available from chemists or health shops. The oils have different properties and effects on us; the various aromas arouse totally different emotions and feelings. They all have antiseptic, tonic or pain-killing properties.

Some aromatherapy uses

- Relaxing baths: use oil of **basil, hyssop** or **geranium** – 2 drops per bath.
- Tired feet – oil of **lavender, rosemary, juniper** – 2 drops of each in 3 litres (5 pints – all Imperial measures U.K.) of water.
- Massage – oil of **marjoram**: 4 drops per 5 cl. (1 fluid oz.) olive or other oil. Oil of **lavender**: 5 drops per 5 cl. (1 fluid oz.) olive or other oil. Oil of **geranium**: 8 drops per 5 cl. (1 fluid oz.) olive or other oil.

● Inhalation – for a head cold: oil of **eucalyptus**: 8 drops in 3 litres (5 pints) water. Oil of **basil**: 2 drops in 3 litres (5 pints) water. Oil of **peppermint**: 2 drops in 3 litres (5 pints) water.

How to make a pomander

1. Take an unblemished fresh orange, lemon or lime. Tie tape round it to separate into four equal segments.
2. Stick the surface with cloves, placing them in rows that touch each other, to cover the orange completely. (Pierce holes first to make this process easier.)
3. Mix up ground cinnamon, nutmeg, cloves, allspice and roll the fruit in this powder. Wrap it in tissue paper and place in a warm, dark place for six to eight weeks.
4. Unwrap, peel off tape.
5. Tie a new ribbon around the orange where tape was, leaving a loop to hang the pomander up. This hanging ornament will give a warm fragrance for many months.

Orris root powder

This is an ingredient in a number of herbal mixtures. The root is of an iris, *Iris florentina*, which has purple, white and yellow-streaked flowers. When dried and powdered the root has a fixative effect on scented mixtures. When fresh the rhizome is practically odourless, but when dried its fragrance resembles sweet violet. It has been used for centuries as a cosmetic additive. The plant is a perennial and grows to approximately 60 cm. (2 ft.) in height.

Pests in the garden

● Slug repellents: bitter herbs will deter slugs and seed-eating birds and mice. Dry, powder and spread the herbs over the ground before seeds are covered, and also sprinkle between plants as an effective deterrent. Try southernwood, wormwood, mugwort (*Artemisia vulgaris* – a wild plant), rue.
● Aphids: garlic grown amongst rose bushes seems to deter aphid infestation without damaging ladybird populations.

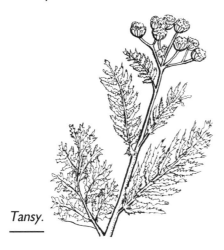

Tansy.

Basil.

Camomile.

- Blackfly: winter or summer savory (*Satureja montana* or *Satureja hortensis*) grown between rows of beans will certainly help to reduce blackfly infestation.
- Rhubarb leaf pesticide: this recipe will kill sap-sucking insects, but beware – do not eat plants for two weeks after spraying:
  1 kg. (3 lbs) rhubarb leaves
  3 litres (5 pints) water
  Boil for an hour and then strain and mix with 100 g. (4 oz.) soft soap. Spray the mixture over offending pests. (Rhubarb leaves are poisonous to people.)
- Another pesticide: mustard (*Brassica nigra*) cut down when in flower, then dug into the ground, will kill soil-borne pests and eggs.

Culinary herbs

Culinary herbs have risen greatly in popularity and there is now a certain market for harvested fresh herbs. Herb growing gardeners could consider marketing fresh cut herbs for sale to local greengrocers, wholefood and health food shops (these latter provided no chemicals have been used in herb production).

Making up batches of fresh 'bouquet garni' is an enterprise worth trying. Perhaps restaurants could be supplied weekly. Evergreen perennial herbs such as rosemary, bay (*Laurus noblis*) and winter savory are easily cultivated; other popular herbs for this purpose could be parsley, sage, mint, and annually grown basil and dill.

Cooking with herbs

1. When experimenting with herbs in cooking, add tiny amounts at first until sure the flavour is acceptable – aim for subtlety.
2. Dominant herbs that do not mix well are: basil, rosemary, oregano, thyme, sage and tarragon.
3. Fresh herbs taste strongest.
4. Avoid cooking herbs too long – add last to a dish and crush before using.

- Bouquet garni: put pinches of dried thyme, marjoram, parsley and bay onto small muslin or cheesecloth squares. Tie up into bags. Add individual bags to savoury stews or casseroles. Can use different combinations of herbs fresh herbs can also be used. Tie a length of thread to the bag for ease of removal.
- Basil (*Ocimum basilicum*): this is a delicate plant with a pungent and evocative odour. It is an annual raised from seed sown indoors in spring; and in May or even June outdoors. Needs a sunny sheltered site. Use in any tomato-based foods, or dishes of Italian origin. The recipe that follows can be added to soup, spaghetti, stews or pizzas and is highly recommended.
  ### 'Pestou'
  3 cloves garlic, 30 g. (1 oz.) fresh basil, chopped finely; 60 g. (2 oz.) fresh grated Parmesan, 4 tablespoons olive oil.

  Pulp or mince up garlic cloves, add basil, keep pounding. Add grated cheese and continue to mix. When mixture is smooth beat in the oil drop by drop. Carry on mixing until left with a smooth greenish paste.

- Dill (*Anethum graveolens*): with a fennel-like appearance, this plant is a delicate annual, sown successively from spring onwards. It can grow up to 1 m. (3 ft.) high. Fresh leaves can be picked and used six weeks after sowing. Will grow well in window boxes.
  ### Dill Salad
  Chopped leaves mixed with thinly sliced cucumber make a delicious salad or sandwich filling.

  Dill can also be added when cooking courgettes. The seeds are used in gripe water as they contain an essential oil with soothing properties.

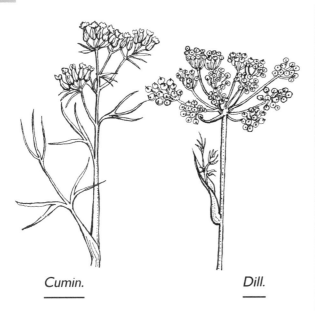

Cumin.   Dill.

- Coriander: a hardy annual, sown outside in spring. The leaves when young have a delightful flavour and can be chopped like parsley. They are especially good in curries and Indian food. The seeds are used in an authentic curry powder.

Fresh chutney
Mix coriander leaves, grated coconut, yoghurt, and a few squirts of lemon juice in a blender, for a really good chutney to complement Indian food.

Herbal oils for cooking
The best herbs for this purpose are: basil, savory, fennel, thyme, rosemary and tarragon. The oils are very effective for marinating meat or vegetables, braising, frying rice, and salad dressings.
Method: Crush chosen fresh herbs with pestle and mortar, put two tablespoons of crushed herbs into a wide-necked screwtop bottle. Fill this three-quarters full with sunflower, corn, vegetable or olive oil. Add one tablespoon of wine vinegar and three or four black peppercorns. Seal bottle tightly and stand it in sun. Leave for two or three weeks, shaking bottle once or twice a day. After this time strain off oil, and discard herbs. Repeat the process with fresh herbs and taste oil to see if it has acquired sufficient flavour.

Herb salts: Crush fresh leaves of any preferred herb plant or plants with sea salt or rock salt using a pestle and mortar or blender. This mixture will keep indefinitely. Similarly research herb butters, herb honey, herb vinegars, herbal wines and brews.

Medicinal herb uses

Infusions. Pour 0.6 l. (1 pt.) of boiling water on to 20–30 g. (about $^3/_4$–1 oz.) of fresh (or dried) herb. Leave this in a stone or china teapot to infuse for 7–10 minutes. Cover to retain the aroma. Strain and serve. Can be sweetened with honey or taken with lemon if desired.

A raised herb garden.

Lemon Verbena

A herbal decoction. This is made by simmering roots and woody parts of a herb for at least ten minutes, to extract their properties. An enamel or stainless steel saucepan should be used. Use 15 g. (1/2 oz.) of the herb to a pint of cold water. Cover, bring to the boil and simmer gently. Strain before drinking.

Tannin-type tea. Leaves of blackberry, raspberry, rose-bay willowherb and strawberry, dried and then used in a tea-like manner make a palatable and less addictive brew than traditional 'cha'.

The preceding plants have a mild restorative effect, and can be defined as being simple (as opposed to compound) remedies for everyday complaints.

Propagation

Most wild herb seed can now be obtained from specialist growers – so please don't reduce wild populations by collecting your own.

Sowing – outside in early April–May. A very fine tilth is necessary. When seed is very fine, fluid drilling may be attempted (a grand name for mixing seed with a cellulose-based wallpaper paste WITHOUT fungicide). Pre-soaking of some seed is necessary and delicate types need pre-sowing in trays.

Wild flower seed should be sown outdoors in the autumn, as many varieties need the cold temperatures of winter to break seed dormancy.

Soft wood cuttings. Take these in late spring or early summer. Ideal for many aromatic shrubby herbs.

● Select vigorous new shoots, 3 or 4 inches long, without flower buds. Pull away from the main woody stem including a small heel of wood.

● Dip in a proprietary rooting compound.

● Strip off lower leaves and insert around the edge of a flower pot containing 50/50 mix peat and sand.

● Covering with a plastic bag often seems to help, but this should be removed regularly for ventilation, and the pot placed in light shade.

Semi-ripe cuttings. These are taken and treated in the same way, but from longer shoots in early autumn. Suitable for rosemary, lemon verbena, bay and myrtle.

Layering. This happens naturally when stems touch the soil and form roots. Many plants have this capacity. It can be stimulated artificially by pegging the stem down into surrounding soil. Early to late summer is the ideal time; new roots form rapidly. Plants that can be propagated in this way are: thymes, marjorams, calamint, winter savory, hyssop.

Some notes on harvesting and storing herbs

1. Correct harvesting leads to successful storage; there is nothing more depressing than uncovering piles of mouldy leaves instead of the fragrant herbs you anticipated.

2. Timing is crucial: collect after dew has dried but avoid hot sunny days. The precious volatile oils tend to evaporate in intense heat.

3. The best time to cut is just before the plants flower, though thyme and rosemary are best taken when in flower. The growing plant needs to recover between each harvest; in the peak growing season, about one third of the plant can be taken at each cut.

4. Use sharp scissors to avoid bruising leaves.

5. Speed in drying is important and a constant draught or stream of warm air most helpful. The herb is best laid to dry in wooden boxes with some kind of loosely woven material stretched over the top of the box and nailed, leaving an air space. Small bunches tied with elastic bands and hung upside down also dry successfully. When herbs are crackly to touch they are ready, but any musty-smelling ones are not.

6. Labelling is important – one dried herb looks much like another and smells may not always be distinctive enough.

7. Light will destroy volatile oil content so it is best to dry herbs in a darkish place.

8. Herbs should be stored in opaque, labelled jars with screw tops. Sweet jars are fine for this if kept in a dark place. Do not mix herbs at this stage unless a mixture is being made. They will usually keep for a year, then should be discarded. Some may be used as a mulch in the garden to deter certain pests.

9. If you wish to collect seed from any herb, cut the plants just before seeds are ready to drop and invert inside a pillowcase or brown paper bag; seeds will collect inside.

10. Freezing – the herbs need blanching first in the same fashion as for freezing vegetables. Plunge into boiling water for one minute then into cold water for two minutes. Dry well before freezing. Pack into polythene bags and label. The herbs can be diced and frozen in ice-cubes.

SIXTEEN

Fruit within reach

Most of us can recall those huge old apple trees dominating the bottom of the garden, where, once a year, the owners brace for the ritual of balancing ladders against the lower branches or else wait for a storm to deliver the crop. Usually the fruit feeds birds and wasps.

This dismal picture is responsible for giving fruit-growing an unnecessary reputation for being difficult, especially if you have restricted mobility. It need not be so. The mature size of the fruit tree depends not on the variety grown, but on the rootstock used. Any variety can be grafted or budded onto a dwarfing rootstock. This, along with methods of training the tree, puts the world of fruit growing within easy reach of most gardeners. In addition, fruit trees grown on dwarfing rootstocks can be suitable for even the smallest garden and can also be grown in containers on patios or balconies.

There is now a range of rootstocks available to allow a wide choice of eventual tree size, form, and rates of growth. Apples, pears and stoned fruit can all be grown in various restricted forms, trained against a boundary wall or fence; or as dividers, trained on wires or fencing between plots or alongside paths. The advantages of specially trained forms are many: easy access; ease of netting, spraying, pruning, thinning and picking.

Popular ways of training fruit trees include the 'cordon', 'espalier' and 'fan' systems, all of which offer advantages for gardeners working from a sitting position or with restricted mobility. The use of long-arm pruners and pickers with light-weight, adjustable handles brings the fruit on these forms well and truly within reach.

Trained forms

There are two main groups of apple and pear varieties: 'tip bearing', where fruit is mainly borne on the end of shoots, and 'spur bearing', where the fruit is carried on short 'spurs' close to the main stem or branch. When training fruit in a restricted way as described below, tip bearers should be avoided. Varieties which are tip bearers include 'Beauty of Bath', 'Laxtons Superb', and 'Worcester Pearmain'. Other fruit – plums, cherries, peaches etc. – aren't such a problem in this respect.

Until recently these stoned fruits have been the province of the largest gardens – not only on account of their size but also because of the need to grow two or three varieties to ensure cross-pollination. Modern, dwarfing rootstocks, as well as the introduction of improved varieties, have changed all this. 'Stella' is an excellent self-fertile variety for fan-trained cherries; 'Victoria' takes a lot of beating for plums, and 'Peregrine' is a good first choice for a peach on a warm, south-facing wall.

*   *   *

A fruit garden within reach.

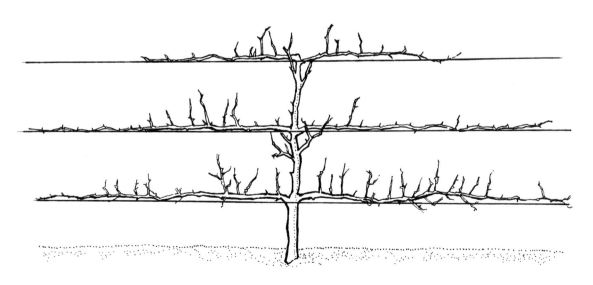

An espalier-trained pear tree.

Training methods explained

Cordons
(suitable for apples, pears and plums)

This is the most common form of restricting the growth of fruit trees. Trees are planted about 1 m. (3 ft.) apart and are trained at an angle of 45° onto supporting wires, fence or wall. The tree is grown as a single stem by cutting back all side shoots to encourage fruiting buds. The height to which the tree is grown depends on your reach, although cordons are rarely grown above 2 m. (6 ft.).

Vertical cordons are a less usual form in which the tree is trained vertically, rather than at an angle.

Prune cordons by cutting back all side shoots in late summer: disregard the small tuft of leaves at base of side shoot, count three leaves along and cut close to the third leaf – never through it. If secondary growth springs from these cuts, cut these back in the autumn to one leaf from their basal tuft.

A maiden tree.

Espaliers
(for apples and pears)

This is a larger version of the cordon, where the main stem is grown vertically, and side shoots are trained horizontally in tiers. Trees are planted 4–5 m. (about 12–15 ft.) apart. Side branches are trained in opposite pairs, spaced at approximately 35 cm. (15 in.) intervals, and the number of tiers depends on your reach.

Prune all shoots from side branches in the same way as described for cutting side shoots from cordons.

Fans

This method is best for the stoned fruit – peaches, plums, cherries, nectarines etc. In effect, it is a development of the espalier method. However, instead of growing the branches horizontally, branches are trained – over a number of years – into a flat 'fan' shape. To describe how this is done is rather like trying to describe, in a few lines, how to knit a jumper! It is far easier to go to the pattern, in this case the description given in fruit growing books. Rest assured – fan training is not as difficult as it sounds!

Other methods of training

There are some other forms in which fruit trees can be grown, which do not offer the same benefits as the above methods if you have restricted mobility, but are still much more accessible than conventional tree forms. They include dwarf bush, spindle bush (or continental spindle) and dwarf pyramid. A useful way of training plums, which often produce a lot of long whippy shoots in their first year, is by hooping. This method involves bending the shoots right down and tying them to the main stem about 30 cm. (1 ft.) from the ground.

All of these restricted forms can be trained by any patient gardener from maiden trees (a single stem comprising one season's growth). These maidens transplant better than the older trees, though older (and more expensive) nursery-trained trees can be chosen for quicker results. Leaf-fall is a good time to plant. As a rough guide cordons need about 1 m. (3 ft.) between trees with 2–3 m. (7–10 ft.) between rows; fans and espaliers 4–5 m. (12–15 ft.) between trees with 2.5–3 m. (8–10 ft.) between rows.

Whichever system you use it is essential to provide a supporting framework of pressure-treated wooden posts 3.5 m. (12 ft.) apart, 2 m. (7 ft.) above ground and 50 cm. (18 in.) set in concrete. For cordons, galvanized wires should span the posts 75 cm. (2½ ft.) above ground level and then at 50 cm. (2 ft.) intervals to the required height. The wires (gauge 10 for the top one and gauge 12 for the others) should pass through holes drilled in the inner posts and be fixed to the end posts with restraining bolts. Use bamboo canes to span the wires at the planting stations. For espaliers, the wires correspond to the number of fruiting tiers planned and should be spaced about 40 cm. (15 in.) apart. Fans are trained on wires 20 cm. (9 in.) apart. If you are growing the trees against a fence or wall, firmly fix the wires along the wall by means of eye-bolts.

Be careful to consider access when planting trees – dry, non-slip surfaces are safest as well as needing little maintenance. If you are confined to a wheelchair, try and design a 'through' route past your trees or else provide a turning space.

Full details on all methods of training and pruning fruit trees are readily available from any good book on fruit growing.

Where to start

1. Decide on the fruit you like. It is possible to grow *more* than one variety on a single rootstock – so you can still have a choice of fruit even with very limited space. Very vigorous growing varieties e.g. 'Bramley' are not worth growing in restricted forms, even on dwarfing rootstocks – they simply put the fruit out of reach!
2. Consider soil type, topsoil depth, soil fertility etc. In poor soil, a more vigorous rootstock may be needed or your tree will grow weak and be a poor cropper.
3. Pollination: do the cultivars you have chosen need other trees for pollination or will they pollinate themselves? This is an essential point as lack of pollination will mean no fruit! Don't forget, neighbours' trees can play a part here.
4. The space you have available, the extent of your reach, and any other limitations.

Soft fruit

The previously described cordon and espalier training systems can be well adapted for growing redcurrants, gooseberries and whitecurrants. Not only do they make the fruit easier to pick – essential for gooseberries – but they also make it easier to protect the crops from birds. (If you enjoy soft fruit, a fruit cage is a good investment.)

Other soft-fruit crops which give a good return for the space they occupy are blackcurrants and raspberries. They enjoy a annual mulch to feed the surface roots and pruning out the old fruiting wood after harvesting. They are largely trouble-free, but do choose the smaller varieties for ease of picking and make sure you buy virus-free stocks. Raspberries flourish in rows at least 1 m. (3 ft.) apart and, tied into supporting wires, up to a height of 2 m. (6 ft.) (or height to suit your reach). A 10 cm. (4 in.) straw mulch helps to keep the weeds down and conserve moisture – important not only for the setting fruit but also for the gardener, as it reduces the watering chores.

Strawberries can also be grown in more accessible ways – plant in raised beds, tubs or special strawberry crocks positioned at a height to suit you.

To sum up, go slowly in designing your soft-fruit garden; remember your limitations – physical, time, experience – and choose plants to provide a succession of fruit, plants which are disease-resistant and fruit to suit the palate.

SEVENTEEN

Hanging gardens

One gardening writer describes hanging baskets as 'moveable miniature gardens, floating in the air or at eye-level; showing off; spilling their contents in all directions!' (*Sheila Howarth – 'Miniature Gardens'*.)

Indoors or out, hanging baskets can be used to great effect: to bring a room alive; to obscure eye-sores; transform ugly corridors; to turn a dull yard into a glowing garden. Planted for seasonal or permanent display, a hanging basket can show off almost any plant of your choice that has a trailing or spreading habit.

Here we consider a range of options for creating successful hanging displays and offer some ways around the common planting and maintenance difficulties experienced by people with limited mobility or other special needs.

Containers:
1. Traditional wire baskets

Plastic-coated with chain attached, these can be relatively expensive to buy and do need lining, but will last almost indefinitely and do not rust.

Linings for this type:

Moss is lovely if available fresh, and if kept damp, retains its freshness. It also looks pleasingly natural, and allows easy planting through the base and sides of the basket.

Black polythene liner inside moss liner – with holes pierced through: helps hold vital moisture, while retaining a 'natural' effect.

Polythene alone – with holes pierced: effective, but only looks good if plants grow over to camouflage.

Papier maché: home-made, using a suitable mould, made from newspaper and flour and water or wallpaper paste (without fungicide).

'Erin'-type liners: made from compressed fibres, totally biodegradable and will last for two years or more. Holes need to be made in sides and base for trailing plants.

Sponge-rubber: light; holds water well.

'Coconut-fibre' matting liners: recently introduced from Australia. Described as 'a woolly-textured, natural-looking coconut fibre, reinforced with latex to prevent the basket drying out, and tough enough to last several seasons'.

2. Plastic baskets

Complete with drip trays and plastic or wire hangers, these are simply plastic pots, in various colours, sizes and styles, readily available from garden centres and shops, and usually cheaper than wire baskets. There are some very small baskets, 15 cm. (6 in.) or so in diameter, in this type, which will dry out in minutes in hot breezy weather, and are probably best used for indoor displays. Plastic baskets can be 'softened' by ample planting with trailing specimens.

3. Macramé hangers

Craft-orientated people could make their own knotted string/twine hangers fairly easily, or they can be bought ready-made to hold any kind of pot or container. Macramé hangers can be used to present a wire hanging basket more decoratively for indoor or conservatory use; or could hold an 'Erin' liner slit to allow side planting. They are often combined with clay pots, allowing planting from the top only.

4. Home-made ideas

● Hanging lemonade bottles can make light-weight plastic bottles ideal for displaying small

A home-made hanging display made from old tights; planted with alpine strawberries.

A covered walkway or pergola ideal for a good display of hanging baskets.

trailers. Large 1–2 gallon plastic containers with tops cut off and holes punched for string can provide chunky hanging pots. Make drainage holes in base, and holes can be cut in the sides for trailers.

- Thread one leg of a pair of tights inside the other; fill with compost to a depth of about six inches; knot the tights to form a mini 'growbag'. Fold nylon back over 'growbag' and knot; repeat for four thicknesses. Cut slits in the bag to plant small trailers.
- Cut a tyre in half to form a semi-circle, make holes at either end and suspend with strong twine. Paint, and line with gravel, fill with compost, plant up.
- Hanging ivy balls are a form of indoor (or small-scale outdoor) 'topiary' display. Use plastic-coated wire to make a suitably shaped base: a ball, cylinder, bird shape or initial. Completely fill the wire shape with sphagnum moss; then insert rooted ivy cuttings (both *Hedera* spp. and *Rhoicissus* spp., or *Ficus pumila*) into it, fixing them into place with u-shaped pieces of plastic-coated wire. As the ivy grows, either weave the shoots through the netting, or tie them in with plastic-coated wire. Some pruning may be needed to encourage shoots to develop in the right directions. Spray the arrangement daily and give the moss a regular soaking – it should never be allowed to dry out. Add liquid fertilizer, during watering or as foliar feed, at fortnightly intervals while the ivy is actively growing.

5. Wall baskets

These also offer scope for presentation of trailing and pendulous plants – ideal in small spaces such as a backyard. Types range from the simplest plant pot which can be fitted into a pot 'gripper' and fastened to a wall or drain pipe, through to wrought iron basket styles, terracotta and stone pots of all kinds, plastic 'window box' types to rest on brackets; wire half-baskets and homemade planters using half tyres.

Points to consider when providing support for hanging/ wall baskets

Firm fixing is vital to avoid disaster. When attaching wall baskets and brackets to solid walls, masonry nails or screws with the correct rawlplugs are essential. To suspend a basket from the

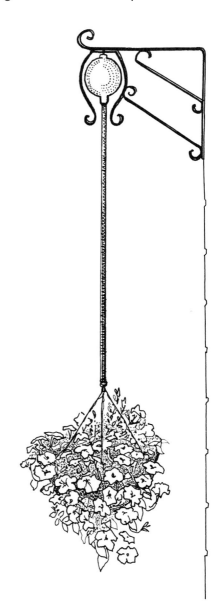

An installed hanging basketline which allows you to raise and lower the basket easily for maintenance.

ceiling, large screw-hooks are suitable, but *only* when the necessary support is provided by a joist or batten.

An accessible height will determine positioning; eye-level or slightly above may be best. Another way to display a hanging basket for easy maintenance is to rest it on top of an old chimney pot or other strong support, rather than suspending it. These 'gardens' need copious watering, feeding, and often dead-heading, so if you choose a position that is higher than eye-level (sitting or standing), a pulley system of some sort may well be necessary (or for those with no mobility/balance/strength problems, a step-ladder) for watering access. An old-fashioned washing-line pulley, firmly fixed to the wall, works well but there are several other gadgets on the market: the 'Hi-lo' attaches to a wall bracket and has a line which can be raised or lowered and locks into positions as required. It supports weights of up to 10 kg. (25 lbs.).

Composts for hanging baskets

The right choice of compost can be crucial to success, and has a direct effect on watering and feeding requirements. Compost with the ability to hold water without becoming waterlogged, and which allows free drainage, while having the ability to retain nutrients, is the ideal.

A heavy soil-based compost such as John Innes No 2 or 3 is superb for plant growth providing excellent nutrition and water-holding properties for plants that will be competing for food and moisture in a very confined space. Plants need less frequent feeding in this type of compost than in peat-based types, and this planting medium also dries out more slowly. It provides free drainage for plants such as geraniums, which prefer this.

Soil-based composts are not as clean to handle as peat-based ones; they are also heavier – which can be very awkward if the basket has to be regularly lowered and raised for watering.

The most readily available (and cheapest) compost is peat-based. This type is perfectly adequate for most needs and relatively light, but does dry out rapidly. Baskets using this type of compost may need watering twice daily in very hot weather, and will certainly require feeding.

Feeding

A slow-release, granular, resin-coated fertilizer is ideal for hanging baskets: e.g., Osmocote Plus, Ficote or Nutricote. This can provide nutrients for at least one season (and up to 18 months) depending on the formulation chosen. The product continually releases small quantities of nutrient in response to soil temperature and moisture content, in line with plant growth requirements. 'Plantpins' also offer a slow-release feeding option. If using a standard fertilizer, Phostrogen is excellent for promoting flowering – applied as a drench every 10 days or so – or for quick results, as a foliar feed (applied as liquid and absorbed mainly by foliage) – but not on days when the sun is shining brightly, as then sun scorching may occur.

- If dripping baskets are a problem – choose a style with a built-in saucer.

Positioning

- Good circulation of air is needed, but not wind tunnel conditions – this will cause battering.
- Fumes from heaters and boilers can cause problems.
- Light – choice of plants is important here – sun-lovers will become leggy and miserable if relegated to a dark corner.

General upkeep

Dead-heading: a simple but effective way to encourage and prolong flowering.

Pests and diseases: as with all gardens, good culture techniques promote good health – even more so in a confined space where plants compete fiercely for available resources.

Powdery mildew: most prevalent in dry weather following a wet spell – even more so in periods of erratic watering. Prevention is easier than cure, so always maintain a regular watering regime.

Aphids: hot drying winds can favour aphid infestation for similar reasons to the above.

Any fungicides and insecticides can be applied using hand-held sprayers. For those who prefer not to mix their own solution, there are a num-

*Any unusual container which can take compost
and plants will provide a talking point. In this
case the container can be used as a hanging
garden.*

ber of ready-mixed proprietary products in easy-
held spray containers. When choosing a sprayer,
try different ones to see which suits you best.

The need for water

The following points may solve some watering
problems:

● Upright watering cans with short spouts can
be heavy and awkward to lift and tilt when
watering hanging baskets. A hose with an adjustable spray nozzle attached is much easier
to use – especially when you have several baskets to water. Another idea is to use a lance on
a pressure sprayer – which minimizes lifting
but requires vigorous pumping.
● If your basket is fixed to a pulley system, it can

simply be lowered and immersed in a bowl of
water for a good soak. Drain the basket well
before raising, and allow to drip onto
newspaper.
● New polymer crystals that absorb up to 400
times their own mass in water and release the
water as the plants require. This drastically
cuts down the need for regular watering.

How to plant up a hanging basket of traditional wire type

1. Rest the basket so that it is stable, and at the
most convenient height for you to plant up.
2. Line with handfuls of moss, then black plastic
– make slits in this to allow for side and base
planting. Crocks may be placed in the base at this

stage if you want to encourage free drainage.

3. Firm compost into the basket: either fill almost completely, or plant and fill as you go – whatever seems easiest.

4. Small trailers can be inserted through the base and sides of the basket so that their roots are firmly embedded, but the foliage is hanging outside.

5. Place plants of upright habit in the centre of the basket with trailers round the outside.

6. Either use young plants and leave space for them to attain maturity, or for an instantaneous effect, plant mature specimens more closely. In the case of seasonal baskets, overplanting will not be hazardous as the intended life span is relatively short.

7. Give a really good soaking and leave somewhere cool for a few days to settle.

8. Hang in final position.

Planting ideas

Outdoors:

Winter/spring: pansies, ivies, miniature bulbs (snowdrops, *Narcissi, Crocus,* tulips, *Iris, Scilla*), *Polyanthus; Myosotis; Arabis; Aubretia* and other spring-flowering trailing alpines.

Summer, sunny sites: 'Cascade' or other trailing geraniums; 'Cascade' *petunias* – like 'Resisto' strain (good in damp weather); *Alyssum; Lobelia: L. tenvior* is dark blue with white eye and trailing habit; mignonette (scented); trailing nasturtiums, e.g., 'Alaska'; *Tropaeolum canariense; Nepeta; Saxifraga spp; Dianthus deltoides; Verbena x hybrida* (almost hardy); *Calceolaria* 'Sunshine'; *Chrysanthemum* – the 'Charm' varieties; *Matricaria; Thunbergia alata* (black-eyed Susan); *Ipomoea* (morning glory); *Lathyrus* (sweet pea); try dwarf varieties such as 'Knee Hi', 'Snoopea' or 'Bijou'; *Helichrysum petiolatum*

(a furry-leaved trailer); *Nemesia strumosa; Oxalis; Mesembryanthemum* and *Portulaca* – these love dry, sunny positions.

Summer, shady sites: *Impatiens* (F1 bedding varieties); trailing *Viola spp;* tuberous *Begonia spp; Euphorbia Myrsinites* (perennial); *Campanula isophylla; Fuchsia;* some types of dwarf *Nicotiana; Coleus; Mimulus; Begonia semperflorens;* fern-like plants: *Corydalis cheilanthifolia, Begonia sutherlandii* (pendulous).

Edible plantings: parsley; the more compact mint species; thymes; strawberries (alpine varieties are best); small round-rooted carrots, dwarf cherry tomatoes, dwarf climbing beans, 'Saladisi' mixtures, 'Saladbowl' lettuce.

Perennials/outdoors: *Alyssum saxatile, Vinca minor* 'Variegata', *Cerastium tomentosum* (all fast growing and evergreen), *Hedera spp; Euonymus fortunei.*

Indoors

Winter: *Schlumbergera bridgesii* – Christmas cactus; *Chlorophytum comosum* (spider plant); *Tradescantia/Hedera/Cissus/Rhoicissus; Tomeia menziesii* (piggyback plant); *Scindapsus aureus/ S. pictus* (dragon's ivy); *Philodendron scandens* (sweetheart ivy); any other trailing indoor foliage plants.

Summer: *succulents, e.g., Rhipsalidopsis rosea* 'Electra', *Schlumbergera gaertneri, Echeveria, Sempervivum* and *Sedum spp;* tuberous (trailing) *Begonia;* ferns – *Nephrolepis* and *Davallia spp, Asparagus plumosus, *Asparagus sprengeri; *Saxifraga stolonifera* (mother of thousands); *Columnea; Browallia; Episcia; Achimenes; *Jasminum polyanthum; Duchesnea; *Helxine; *Tolmeia; Plectranthus; Maranta; Hoya; *Setcreasea purpurea.* **Outdoors also, in sunny summer sites.**

When space is at a premium, raised beds or containers are often the only solution for would-be growers! They can widen the horizons in even the most restricted urban settings.

EIGHTEEN

Beautiful, bountiful balconies

Flat-dwellers often have a balcony – if only a small one – and on sunny days it is common to see people sitting outside, sometimes many storeys up, enjoying the view and the sunshine. There is now a trend towards using these small outdoor areas as growing space for plants, providing colour, interest, and often a useful addition to the kitchen table – a familiar practice in southern Europe for centuries. The result is a high-rise garden that gives delight to the residents, neighbouring flat-dwellers and passers-by below.

If you're keen to make the most of a balcony or other small growing space – whether at home or in an institutional setting – these tips may help your ideas to blossom.

A few considerations

Most balconies offer little protection from the elements, lacking the screens and buffers provided by trees, shrubs, hedges and fences in ground-level gardens. Strong winds, and the air turbulence often created between tall buildings, can cause havoc in high-level gardens.

Various types of trellis or netting can be used as wind-breaks to make the balcony more pleasant to sit out on and to provide support for climbing plants. Netlon is one of the best known names in horticultural netting, producing a wide range of types for different purposes. Choose a strong net in the smallest mesh size available, as the larger the mesh the less effective it is as a wind-break. Resist the temptation to build a solid

barrier which could cause severe air turbulence and damage the plants almost as badly as direct wind. Remember, too, to fix the netting securely, especially if you intend growing plants up it. The extra wind resistance produced by the foliage could make your wind-break into a 'sail' which could rip off if not firmly fitted.

Because many flats rise above the city dust level the sun can be as bright and clear on a balcony as in the country. However, total sunlight hours per day can be restricted – in some cases with sunlight only striking the balcony from one side. To increase the light intensity and to provide a more even distribution of light, paint the walls on all sides of the balcony matt white.

It is unlikely that you will want to transport too many tons of soil up to your aerial garden, but it might be an idea to seek advice on the amount of weight your balcony can take and keep a close eye on the materials used for containers and the quantity and type of compost used. (Peat-based composts are lighter than soil-based ones, but dry out more quickly.)

Pots and containers

The most suitable size for a pot or container depends on the space available and the plants you want to grow. The main disadvantages in using small containers are that they dry out quickly and the nutrients in the compost are soon used up. Some plants, such as stonecrops and houseleeks, grow quite happily in small pockets of soil and seem no worse for frequent drying out, but these are exceptions. Most plants soon die if allowed to become completely dry, or at best become more prone to attack by pests and diseases. For choices of containers and details on the different materials see Chapter 5.

Dripping water can be a nuisance to the people on the balcony beneath, so use saucers under your pots wherever you can, and never place pots where they can be knocked or blown into the street below.

Maximizing your growing area

This is what the developers did when they designed high-rise apartment blocks, and the balcony gardener needs to think along similar lines!

Climbing plants such as ivies (*Hedera spp*), climbing hydrangea (*Hydrangea petiolaris*), Virginia creeper (*Parthenocissus*), honeysuckle (*Lonicera*) and clematis (e.g., *Clematis montana*) are perennials which can be planted in pots and containers on the balcony floor and will cover a support quite quickly to produce a vertical garden. The ivies and honeysuckles like shade and will do well next to the wall, even under a deep overhang. Nasturtiums, sweet peas, morning glory, runner beans and some types of culinary pea will give rapid growth for just one season.

The walls of your balcony can also be put to good effect with wall-baskets and strong shelves to support flower pots. Make sure that they are firmly attached, using screws and rawlplugs or sleeve bolts rather than masonry nails. These raised containers are suitable for trailing bedding plants such as geraniums, petunias and lobelia, or for the smaller fruiting (cherry) tomatoes. Gourds, peas and french beans can also do remarkably well in these containers if they get enough light. Traditional hanging baskets can be effectively planted too – providing spectacular curtains of colour until well into the autumn. Fix the hanging baskets onto a pulley system for ease of maintenance.

The railings of the balcony can act as extremely useful supports for climbing plants. A row of troughs or growbags along their base will provide sufficient growing medium for an excellent crop of tomatoes or ridge (outdoor) cucumbers. Peas and runner beans will also do

well in this position, as will a vast array of sun-loving, flowering plants.

Choosing plants

When buying bedding or vegetable plants for your containers, hanging baskets or pots, take care to choose only those which are strong-growing and bushy. Do not be tempted to buy those offered for sale too early in the year as they will be killed by cold winds or have their tender leaves torn to shreds. Choose dark-green bushy plants which are not overcrowded in their trays and avoid those which are yellow or which are already showing flower buds. It is worth the extra expense of buying perennial bedding plants such as geraniums and dahlias which have been grown singly in pots. Inspect perennial plants such as shrubs and climbers to ensure that they are not damaged or diseased, or pot-bound, and have no pests on them.

Planting

Many garden centres sell shrubs and climbers in 'polybags', and it is important to remove these, most easily by cutting with scissors, before planting or potting up.

Points to consider

- If a plant with dry compost around its roots is planted out even into moist surroundings the chances are that the compost will always remain dry and the plant will not grow as it should. Always water or soak your plants before planting them into a larger container.
- Make the hole in the compost large enough to take the roots of the plant easily. Allow the roots room to spread out comfortably once planted in the pot.
- When filling the hole, shake the plant gently up and down so that the compost falls between the roots. Firm the compost with your knuckles so that the wind doesn't rock the plant about. Try to keep the plants at the same level as they were in their boxes or pots, as a change in soil level could cause the stems to rot.

- When planting has been completed, water the plants thoroughly using a fine rose on your watering can. This will not only moisten the compost but will settle the plants in.
- One way of achieving a succession of colour in the containers is to fill them with moist peat and then plunge the plants, still in their pots, into this. As the flowers fade or the plants die the pots can be replaced with others.

Aftercare

In order to prolong the flowering period of decorative plants, dead-heading is an essential, regular activity. Weeding should not be a problem if sterilized compost is used, but feeding the plants with correctly diluted liquid fertilizer will be necessary from six weeks after planting. It is normally necessary to feed plants in containers once or twice a week once established. Watering may well be necessary every day in the summer months. The best time to water is in the evening, so that the plants will have the benefit of the water all night before the sun dries them out again. Perennial plants, including shrubs, will also need watering during the winter. If plant pots are resting on saucers, make sure that they are not standing in water for long periods, as this can kill roots by restricting oxygen availability.

The courtyard garden

One characteristic common to most courtyards is a shortage of soil, but with the use of inexpensive containers even the most depressing backyard can be transformed into an attractive garden area.

First of all, assess your site. Start by standing with your back to the house and study the view, trying to decide which features are worth preserving and which should be screened or removed. It may be expensive to replace or repair damaged flooring but walls can be rapidly and cheaply smartened up with the application of a light-coloured exterior paint. This will immediately increase the amount of reflected light and also destroy hibernating pests in the wall crevices.

Ugly features can be screened by climbing plants. Wooden or plastic trellis fixed in front of walls will support a wide range of plants, including climbing roses, clematis, honeysuckles, climbing nasturtiums, sweet peas, jasmine and runner beans. Try to position the trellis an inch away from the wall to maximize air movement between leaves and facilitate tying. Where a paving stone is lifted to make a small planting area, leave a 25 cm. (10 in.) gap between plant roots and nearby walls to prevent plants from drying out too quickly.

Window boxes can be arranged along a wall to give a cheerful display and contrast pleasantly with the shapes of hanging baskets.

To provide a maintenance-free 'grass' effect between paving slabs or under bushes, grow *Helxine* ('mind your own business' or 'baby's tears') which grows prolifically outdoors – especially in cool, moist situations. It is easy to establish, using very small pieces which root and spread like a weed. Keep a pot full of stock plants of this variety inside during the winter, in case there is a spell of extreme cold, which may kill this attractive ground-cover plant.

Odds and ends of containers and garden furniture can be exploited to show off plants to their best effect. Dark corners can be highlighted with tubs full of flowers, and strawberry pots, horse troughs, sinks and old chimney pots are just some ideas for containers. A large old mirror fixed to a wall behind a colourfully planted container gives an impression of increased size and depth. The frame of the mirror can be softened by a creeper growing up a concealed trellis.

By necessity, courtyards often house drains, coal bunkers and dustbins. Thoughtfully placed flower boxes with wooden trellis firmly tacked to posts will provide sufficient root hold and support for climbers – perhaps a range of different plants growing together in one box – and provide excellent cover.

A small conifer in a container can also be used to break up the regular outline of utility areas behind. Even fairly tall shrubs and trees – up to 3 m. (10 ft.) high – can be grown in containers such as wooden boxes, as long as sufficient nutrients and water are made available, and the yard is fully protected from winds.

By being adventurous and imaginative the darkest and most depressing area can be transformed into an area full of charm and beauty. The value of scented plants in a courtyard setting shouldn't be forgotten . . . the warm sheltered environment contains the fragrances, providing a delightful concentration of scents to enjoy, particularly at dusk. Whether you concentrate on scented plants, or cool, relaxing foliage, or a riot of red geraniums, the well-defined boundaries of the courtyard garden guarantee maximum enjoyment and benefit from a limited amount of work.

NINETEEN

Using and caring for house plants

Any interior, from a clinical bathroom to a gleaming, hot common room can be improved by well-chosen and well-placed plants. An additional dimension will be given to the room, bringing it new life and freshness. But if you don't know how to look after them, house plants can be very disappointing. Read on for our good house plant guide.

Many plant collections develop in a haphazard way, often through spontaneous buys or gifts. The resulting variety is not without charm, but problems can be caused if the wrong plants are kept together or if plants are kept in unsuitable parts of the room. It is also worth considering whether watering will be a problem over long summer weekends.

Plant groups

The continental practice of grouping together many plants to create the effect of an indoor garden has recently become very popular in many countries. The visual effect and difference in atmosphere between a row of demure Busy Lizzies on a windowsill and a boisterous clump of *Ficus benjamina, Ficus radicans, Sparmannia* and *Chlorophytum* is amazing. But there are practical reasons for grouping plants too. Those needing similar conditions and environment really do seem to do much better when set close together. Maintenance, such as spraying and watering, is in one spot and the plants make a micro-climate around themselves, each leaf con-

tributing towards the desired levels of humidity. Low-growing plants needing dappled sunlight can be shaded by the taller plants and in this way ideal growing conditions can be provided.

A group of plants can also be used to make a leafy dividing screen in a large open-plan room. Smaller-scale groups fill in awkward-shaped niches in the room, or perhaps occupy an empty fireplace during the summer months. Suitable large plants tolerating a low light level and low humidity include *Monstera, Ficus, Schefflera* and *Sparmannia* while at the other end of the scale are asparagus fern, *Peperomia, Sansevieria* and *Asplenium.*

Trays and troughs

A natural development of growing plants singly, but grouping them together, is to plant them collectively in a single container. Of course, that makes it essential to choose plants which need similar conditions. For instance, it would be foolish to plant a fern which likes shade with a chrysanthemum which likes sunshine.

Plants should also have practically the same rate of growth. If not, one could swamp the rest and steal all the moisture and nutrients. For small troughs slow-growing species such as African violets should be chosen. Drainage in the container is essential for a permanent or semi-permanent planting. If there are no holes in the container's base, then drill some, or add gravel

As an attractive alternative to single pot plants, two or more plants requiring similar growing conditions will thrive together in a roomy container.

and charcoal, as one would when planting up a bottle garden. This will help to keep the compost sweet and reduce the chance of algae growth.

Plant up in a good open compost, which can be soil- or peat-based, allowing plenty of space between plants for growth and spread. The surface of the compost can be decorated with granite chippings or pebbles and this helps prevent splashing during watering too. Do not over-water: overwatering will kill not just one plant in this instance but your whole collection.

Plants tend to grow rapidly in these conditions and need pruning from time to time. This and replanting are best done in spring and early summer when the quick-growing plants look as if they are outstripping their neighbours.

Temperature, light and shade

When plants make sugar from carbon dioxide and water they use light as their energy source. Hence the name PHOTOSYNTHESIS. The green chlorophyll in the plant's leaves and stems assimilates the light rays and releases oxygen into the air as a waste product. If it is not used at once by the plant, the sugar is converted into starch and stored in the roots. Photosynthesis can only take place during the daytime unless the plant is growing in artificial light conditions. No light at all will kill a plant and poor light will prevent some species from flowering. As a guide, try to provide plants with the light conditions which they experience in their natural habitat. For example *Arums*, palms, ferns and *Aspidistra* do well in quite poor light. *Chlorophytum*, *Dracaena*, *Fatsia*, *Ficus*, *Fittonia* and *Tradescantia* like a reasonable light source. Busy Lizzies, geraniums, *Gloxinia*, all succulents and cacti prefer very bright light.

Remember to turn your plants from time to time. Plant leaves and stems tend to face and grow towards the light, and if left alone will become very lopsided. Obviously in a glasshouse this doesn't happen as the light stimulus is equal all around the plant, but it will happen on a window ledge.

Next to lighting, the most important factor for your plants will be the temperature. Once again, think of where the plant grows in the wild. Humidity is a relevant factor here, especially with larger-leaved plants which can lose a lot of water through transpiration in hot, dry conditions. As a general rule a constant room temperature of 18°–21°C (64°–70°F) is ideal for most house plants, while temperatures of above 24°C (75°F) may cause problems for some plants unless they are in full light and provision is made to increase the humidity of the air around them.

Draughts are fatal to plants. These chilly streams of air come from obvious places such as ill-fitting windows and doors, but watch out, too, for drying convection currents from hidden heat sources. These can originate from washing machines, electric or gas cookers, refrigerators and deep-freezes. Surprisingly, these can dehydrate plants as effectively as direct heat from an open fire, or hot air from an air conditioning vent.

Watering

Watering causes problems for many people, some even refusing to do it, while others give the plants so much water and so often that the roots die due to lack of air in the soil. Regrettably it is not possible to be dogmatic about how much water a plant should have since there are many influencing factors. Plants are affected by their position, the time of year, temperature, the kind of compost used and even the type of flowerpot.

Plants on a sunny windowsill or in a strongly heated room will need more water than plants in a shady, humid bathroom or kitchen. The ferns, which have evolved to live in woodlands or near streams, will require more moisture than the cacti and succulents which are adapted to desert conditions.

Unless you know the requirements of your house plants already, check their pots daily to see if the compost is dry or moist. This can be done by inserting a knife or pencil into the soil and seeing if it emerges moist or sticky. With experience, you can test with your forefinger or by assessing the weight of the pot. Some gardeners claim that a terracotta flowerpot with moist compost in it sounds dull when rapped with a pencil, whereas dry compost gives it a ringing tone.

Terracotta pots tend to dry out more quickly than the plastic types due to their porous nature. They do, however, have the advantage of their weight which helps them to be more stable and less likely to be knocked over.

Do not let your plants dry out and wilt, and avoid over-watering, too. Fine timing is required. Many people try to compromise by watering frequently in minute amounts. This is not a good idea because it causes the surface of the compost to become wet, often with moss or

Diagram showing the main sources of draughts in the kitchen.

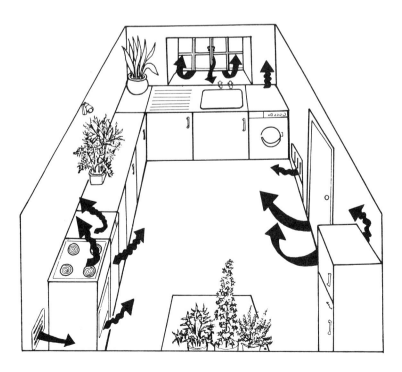

algae growth, while the compost lower down is bone dry. If the compost is dry all through, immerse the pot in a bowl of water to soak. The air in the compost will be displaced by the water and will bubble to the surface. When all the air has floated out, place your potted plant on a flat surface to drain before returning it to its original position.

Most people place their plants in saucers to collect the moisture that drains through the soil. However, do not be tempted to allow your plant to stand in a puddle as this will lead to root-rot. Plants needing a constantly humid atmosphere (such as ferns) benefit most if their pots are plunged into a larger container packed with moist peat, or the pot can be stood on top of pebbles or gravel in a saucer containing water.

If your plants tend to be left untended over long summer weekends and holidays, try using a wick system for watering. A tape or bandage with one end in a bowl of water and the other end pushed into the compost draws up water by capillary action, and delivers it to the plant. Similarly, a bandage attached to a dripping tap at one end and draped over a row of pots in a sink or bath is a good way of keeping moist compost that is already wet. Neither method will be of much help to plants growing in compost that is dry to start with. There are self-watering devices that you can buy, of course, most of them made of porous terracotta, and often in the shape of frogs. A hollow 'spike' is pushed into the compost and the 'frog' reservoir is filled with water. A regulated amount of water is allowed to drain into the compost each day for up to three weeks. Larger self-watering containers can be bought from most garden centres, and these are ideal if you can afford them.

TWENTY

Water in your garden

Water, water, see the water flow ... it's something we all enjoy whether it's still and deep in a pond or quickly moving in a stream or a fountain. To splash the water, see reflections or notice the goldfish is a perennial fascination which enhances the attraction of any garden. And modern methods of construction can bring water features within the reach of most budgets. Read on.....

Ponds

These are the most common and most versatile ways of bringing water into the garden; but before you dig the hole there are a few points you need to keep in mind.

Siting

The siting of a pond or water feature is a major determinant for its use.

A water feature that has to support plant and animal life should be sited in an area that receives plenty of sunlight. Sometimes shelter from the sun during the hottest part of the day will be needed by the fish. Try to provide this by planting suitable specimen plants in and around the pond. Do not site your pond too near overhanging trees, especially deciduous trees. This not only provides too much shade, but can be very harmful. Some leaves, when rotting in water, can produce gases which are harmful – even fatal – to fish. Also, the removal of the fallen leaves is a tiresome job. If it is likely that, during the autumn, leaves will blow into your pond, put netting across it.

Access

Poor access to a water feature can put a limit on the amount of enjoyment you get from it. Think about the surrounding area. If it is all grass, you may find access difficult if you use a wheelchair or walking aid. Is there a site in your garden that will enable you to have access all the way around your water feature? How near will you be able to get in safety?

A raised pond could be a better choice than one set in the ground for not only do you want full access for enjoyment, you will also need to do a bit of maintenance at least annually.

If you have a ground-level pond, try not to build the surrounding banks too high. Leave suitable areas between planting for access right up to the water, to save having to lean or bend over too much to get a good view. You could have a slightly sloping beached area. If you had the time, and were so inclined, you could put a boardwalk going into the pond. A handrail on one or both sides and a gate or a bar at the end of the boardwalk is a useful safety feature.

Construction

The choice is almost limitless! The main factors to consider are costs and time to build. These will depend upon the type of materials used to construct the feature.

There are three main types of material that can be used for pond construction. These are: (a) sheet liners, (b) pre-moulded pools, and (c) concrete. There is also another type of liner available called Bentonite clay.

Many garden centres, especially those specializing in water gardens, will be able to advise on the best type of liner for your pond and pocket. Many recent developments in the manufacture of a better-quality PVC liner give greater scope when choosing the liner. Shop around or send off for a few brochures before making your final decision.

Polythene

Polythene is the cheapest type of liner on the market. It is available in different colours and is readily available from larger stores, DIY merchants and garden centres. The life of polythene is relatively short as it deteriorates in the ultra-violet (UV) rays of the sun. This can be reduced by purchasing polythene that contains a UV inhibitor. In all cases the smallest amount of polythene should be exposed to direct sunlight by keeping the water topped up and the edges covered by stones, shingle or soil, etc.

PVC

PVC liners are more middle-of-the-range in price. They have a much longer life than polythene – usually the top range of PVC is guaranteed for ten years.

Butile

Many people still opt for butile rubber liners. They are very strong and usually have the longest guaranteed life of about 15 years. However, they can be quite costly.

The style of water should always match its surroundings. Here an informal pool matches the setting of a wildlife garden.

A raised water feature enabling a person in a wheelchair to get close to the water.

Concrete

This is considered by some to be the best type of lining for a pond. Concrete is quite versatile and can be moulded into just about any shape. If the mixture and the laying of the concrete is done correctly, the lining will last for a long time and can be compared with butile in this respect. It can be a bit expensive, and don't forget that although mixing concrete is quite straightforward, it can also be very hard work!

Bentonite clay

This could be called a 'living' liner. This comprises small particles of clay which have the ability to absorb six times their own dry weight. In doing so, they swell to become twelve and a half times their original size. When mixed correctly and applied to the site, the clay blocks up the gaps between the soil particles and forms a natural seal. The big advantage with Bentonite clay is that if the seal is punctured at any time the clay expands and gels together and repairs the puncture.

Pre-moulded ponds

These come in all shapes and sizes, and with ready-made shelves at different depths. When considering a pre-moulded pond, there are a few points to take note of. Firstly, decide what you want as your end result. If, for instance, you want a waterfall or rock pool surrounded by plants, you may be limited in the type of plant life and fish that you can have. Some pre-moulded pools are too shallow to support fish or plant life. You may want the very pleasing sight, sound and feel of moving water. However, if you would like a pond for plants and fish, then still water may be better.

When choosing the pond, consider the material the pond is made from. They are usually moulded from glassfibre or plastic. The plastic pre-moulded ponds are cheaper than glassfibre. They are lightweight and durable. You may find they are much more flexible than glassfibre and therefore difficulties could arise when you come to install them.

The price of glassfibre may make you think twice before buying, but it is much more solid than plastic. If you were considering a raised pool, glassfibre would probably be a better choice.

Regardless of the type of pre-moulded pond you buy, check the width of the shelves. Sometimes in mass production, this is not always considered and the shelves can be too narrow to take plants.

Bog Gardens

If you have the room and want something that is a bit more down-to-earth, how about a bog garden? This is simply a saturated area of soil. A little different, it will give you plenty of interest as well as providing a new habitat in your garden. It is also very easy to construct. This may be a consideration if you have difficulty in movement.

This is what you do

Choose site and rough size. Take out soil to a depth of roughly 50 cm. (18 in.). Remove any obvious sharp stones, glass, etc. Line hole with plastic sheeting. Fill with equal parts of peat and loam. Allow this mixture to settle for a few days before planting.

Some alternatives for water gardens

One of the most popular alternatives to building a pond is the half beer-barrel. These are now available from most garden centres and range in price and size. You may even be able to get an old one from a local brewer.

Plant a wildflower water-barrel!
Marginals like marsh Marigold (centre back), bog Bean (front left), and brooklime (front right) frame the delicate water plant common water crowfoot.

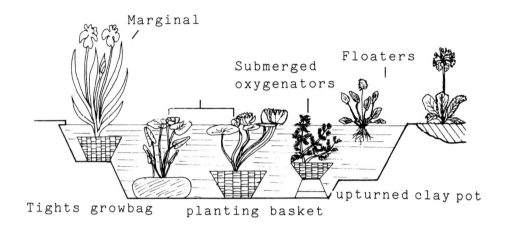

The different types of plants for the water garden feature.

Remember that the barrel needs to be thoroughly clean and watertight. Fill the barrel with water and keep it topped up until the wood swells. It will save time and mess if you test the barrel first. If you buy the barrel from a garden centre, but have difficulty in transporting it home, they can usually make arrangements for delivery – but there may be a delivery charge.

Once the barrel is clean and watertight, place it *in situ*. Put in about 15 cm. (5 in.) of a heavy loam. Create different levels in the barrel by placing in large stones or bricks in-filled with the loam. Topdress the loam with shingle or pea grit to stop fish burrowing for food and fill nearly to the top with water. Do this with care to prevent the water going cloudy. Allow any residue in the water to settle before putting in water snails and fish.

A less expensive version of this is to use a plastic drum. Again, make sure it is clean, free from chemical residues and does not have any cracks in it. You may need to cut it down to a size that suits you better, particularly if you need to sit down to garden.

The outside of the drum can be disguised with a textured paint or an all-weather coloured paint. Then proceed as before.

Don't forget that a water garden can be made out of just about any watertight container. However, try to use a container that is at least 20–30 cm. (8–12 in.) deep.

Another alternative water feature that is becoming very popular is the small free-standing fountain. The varieties of fountains and miniature cascades for indoor and outdoor use are almost endless.

A pond in your garden will greatly benefit wild-life, attracting birds, amphibians and insects, many of which, such as toads and dragonflies, are dependent on water for part of their life cycle.

By careful planning – planting native wild-flowers, shrubs and small trees near the margins (but beware the leaves) – you will provide a haven for animal and plantlife, as more and more natural habitats are lost. It's certainly true that what's good for wildlife is good for people too.

But one note of warning – ponds can be a danger to small children. A toddler can drown in just a few inches of water. A fence around the pond or a submerged guard netting may save much worry.

Some plants:

Aquatic
Aponogeton – water hawthorn
Nuphar – yellow water lily
Nymphaea – water lily
Nymphoides – water fringe

Submerged oxygenators
Ceratophyllum – hornwort
Hottonia – water violet
Myriophyllum – water milfoil
Potomogeton – pondweed

Marginals
Acorus – sweet flag
Caltha palustris – marsh marigold
Iris laevigata
Juncus pseudacorus 'Variegata'
Mimulus – musk
Typha – reed mace

Floaters
Azolla – fairy moss
Stratiotes – water soldier
Utricularia – bladderwort

Bog plants
Astilbe – false goat's beard
Ferns
Hostas
Iris sibirica
Iris kaempferi
Mentha aquatica – watermint
Mimulus – musk
Primula
Trollius – globe flower
Zantedeschia – arum lily

A root-top garden.

A covered fishtank used as a terrarium.

TWENTY ONE

Winter gardening activities

Gardening in winter can be difficult and even unpleasant, unless you have sufficient shelter from the rain and cold wind. But, drawing on the experience of those who are homebound all the year round, we discover a wealth of gardening activities that can give hours of fun and interest in the warmth and comfort of our homes. Here is an outline of just a few of those items that will keep frustrated gardeners busy on the wettest and coldest of days.

A root-top garden

Have you noticed how quickly root vegetables such as turnips, parsnips and carrots grow fresh young leaves when you leave them in a warm kitchen for a few days? The warmth and humidity soon stimulate the plants into growth, believing that spring has arrived. As only a small reserve of stored food is necessary for the leaf buds to produce this growth, you can make use of this tendency to make a 'fern-garden' on a very small scale and at no expense. If you are using kitchen throw-aways make sure that they are fresh and try to include a variety of vegetables. The bits you need are the trimmings from the top of the root. The slices which include the buds need to be at least 1 cm. ($^1/_2$ in.) thick. Garden vegetables will need their leaves trimmed back, but shop-bought produce usually comes cut back already.

The items you need for the garden are a shallow dish or saucer, washed pebbles or stones,

water, and your vegetable tops. Just arrange the tops on the dish, position the pebbles around them and pour the water to half the depth of the slices. In a warm, light place the garden soon takes on a charming fern-like appearance and you can watch the roots growing out and exploring the spaces between the stones. Although you will not get a second crop of vegetables this way it is possible to get a well established and luxuriant garden by giving top-ups of very diluted liquid feed. A few lumps of charcoal in among the pebbles will help prevent algae growth in the water.

Terrariums and plant cases

Growing plants in glass cases is popular these days, particularly with people who live in the hot, dry atmosphere of centrally-heated homes. The reason is that inside the container a humid micro-climate is built up that, with the heat, suits plants whose natural home might be the rain forest or jungle. In fact, inside the terrarium you have a nearly self-supporting community with all the essentials for plant (and some animal) life being cycled and recycled continually. Water from the potting compost at the bottom of the terrarium is taken in by the root-hairs, carried up the plant and evaporates through the leaves. Along with the water evaporated directly off the compost, this condenses on the glass or plastic of the container to run back into the soil. The air in the terrarium also remains in balance. The plants absorb oxygen and give out carbon dioxide at night, and during the day they use carbon dioxide to make sugar and give off oxygen.

Even in a completely sealed container a collection of plants can thrive with almost no attention. On the other hand, a case which is open to the air will need some watering, even though this will be considerably less frequent than ordinary potted plants require. Some people use open-topped containers like fish tanks or goldfish bowls but these are not really terrariums unless a glass (or clingfilm) cover is put over the top.

The container that you have chosen will host your plants for a considerable period of time – probably years – so it needs to be sterile to start with. Wash it out thoroughly with warm water and washing-up liquid, remembering that the glass may not be heat-proof and could crack if put into hot water. Rinse it in clean water and allow it to drain and dry off before putting a layer of charcoal pieces in position on the terrarium base. The depth of this layer is dependent upon the size of your terrarium. For example, in a sweet jar a quarter inch is sufficient whereas in a carboy 5 cm. (2 in.) may be necessary. Soil can be added next, preferably in the form of a fairly dry, weak potting mixture. John Innes and peat-based types mixed with coarse sand are suitable.

If you are using a carboy or demijohn try pouring the compost in through a cardboard funnel and level off using a plastic picnic spoon taped to a length of bamboo cane. This will easily fit in through the narrow mouth and neck of the jar allowing the compost to be evenly spread and holes to be dug for the planting. The depth of soil varies, of course, with the size of container but as a guide 4 cm. (1½ in.) in a sweet jar and 8 cm. (3 in.) in a carboy will be about right.

Planting your terrarium is the most enjoyable part of all. It is best to choose slow-growing plants so that you can put them fairly close together to start with. With the narrow-necked jars you will need to lower the plants down gently on the end of a cotton thread, placing them with a cane and cutting the thread near the plant with a scalpel taped to a stick, or with a razor blade inserted into the split end of a cane. The short length of thread left around the plant will do no harm at all. Packing the compost into place around a plant can be done with a cotton

reel firmly pushed onto the reverse end of your planting cane.

Once established, a terrarium requires little more than light, warmth and a periodic inspection to check that all is well. Remember, however, to place it out of direct sunlight or the temperature inside the container will rise to an unhealthy level and create excessive condensation.

A miniature desert

The ability of cacti to withstand intense heat, cold and drought makes them able to tolerate quite terrible treatment from the laziest gardener and still produce flowers when they are finally given a bit of attention. Succulents have similar endearing qualities but their anatomy is different. They have true leaves like other plants but they are covered in cutin; a waxy, waterproof layer, to conserve water which is stored inside the leaves rather than in the stem. They need plenty of light and, like the cacti, can take a lot of neglect and punishment without complaint. Varieties such as *Echeveria, Aloe* or *Kalanchoe* may produce beautiful flowers but many are grown for their delightful leaf and stem forms, like the popular *Sansevieria* (mother-in-law's tongue) and *Crassulas*.

Grown individually, cacti and succulents give an interesting display but to see the strange shapes to the best advantage they need to be grown in contrasting groups. The containers used for this need only be simple, but good drainage is essential if your planting is to be long term. For short term planting, e.g., in a soup tureen or pottery bowl, adequate drainage can be provided by putting a 4 cm. (1½ in.) mixed layer of pebbles and charcoal at the base. The compost, too, must be free-draining and proprietary types are available in garden centres. If you make your own compost, mix equal parts of sterilized garden soil, coarse silver sand and peat, adding half a teaspoonful of powdered chalk or crushed egg shell to each 15 cm. (7 in.) pot-full of compost that you make. Neither cacti nor succulents need much nutrient so no base fertilizer is necessary. A little liquid feed in the spring and summer will provide all the elements they need for healthy growth and flowering.

When planting a cactus or succulent bowl try to think ahead. Will you be changing your design soon, or will you be leaving it to establish over a period of years? If the planting is to be a temporary display plant fairly closely, but otherwise give plenty of room. In either case do not overcrowd the plants as this prevents air circulation and also lets any pests spread easily. It is best to use a few large stones to fill in the gaps: these can be removed as the plants grow. The surface of the compost between the plants should be scattered with chippings or Cornish grit which is readily available from garden centres. This not only enhances the appearance of the garden by providing a light-coloured background to the plants, but also ensures that the 'neck' of the plant at soil level does not remain wet after watering, which would cause rot.

Correct summer watering of cacti is essential (winter watering is easy: don't do it). In the wild, cacti send their roots out over a wide area, but when they are grown in a pot or some other container, these are forced to go downwards. It is important, therefore, to water thoroughly when it is necessary rather than giving a little at a time. In this way the water will reach the deep young roots, and moss and algae will not be encouraged to grow on the surface soil which very frequent watering makes sour.

The siting of your garden is important too. The two main needs are bright light and air. Both these are readily available in a desert, as they also are on most window ledges, especially if there are radiators or convector heaters immediately adjacent to them. The hot air from these will set up convection currents, which ensure a continuous passage of new air over your garden. These window ledges may also become quite cold at night when the central heating turns itself off. This, too, is an advantage as it is during these cold periods that cacti and succulents make the buds which give rise to such a startling display of flowers in the summer.

Although cacti and succulents can take all the punishment that the most negligent gardener is likely to throw at them, there are two pests which can spoil your garden. The worst of these is the mealy bug, which is a small grey-white insect with a woolly coat, and the other is the scale insect, which is pale brown and looks like a small drop of wax. They can be killed with malathion, but even the corpses of these insects are unsightly. It is best to remove both types with a pipe cleaner or cotton wool swab dipped in methylated spirit. Spraying or watering with insecticide will prevent the pests from establishing in the first place.

Cacti and succulents can sometimes go down to diseases which are generally caused by fungi. The main sign is a brown spongy patch which is normally the outward sign that the plant is already rotten inside. There is no real cure for this but it is fairly easy to prevent by good culture – in particular, by hiding the watering-can during the late autumn and winter. On the whole, however, these plants are amazingly trouble-free and can give a great deal of pleasure and entertainment for a very small amount of trouble.

A miniature desert.

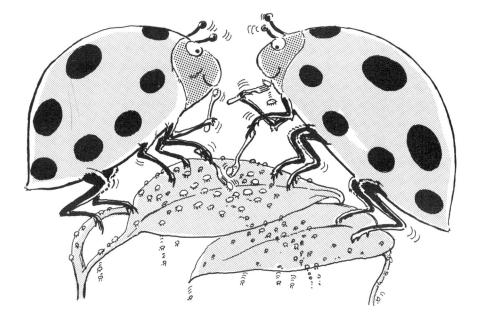

TWENTY TWO

Pest control the organic way

You don't have to be committed to organic growing to take advantage of the pest-control methods outlined in this chapter. Avoiding the use of conventional chemical pesticides will not entitle you to call your produce 'organically grown', it is just one requirement amongst several others needed for a truly 'organic' crop. Nonetheless, it is common for horticulturists in the field of horticultural therapy to reject the often quick and effective chemical solutions to pest problems in favour of an organic approach. Here are some methods in current use and the reasoning behind this gentler line of attack.

Safety: gardeners who use pesticides regularly are often concerned that they or others may come into accidental contact with chemical pesticides. In most cases, pesticides are only handled by users, and chemicals are locked away when not in use – so the chance of someone swallowing, or being splashed with chemicals is small. There is a greater risk, though, of eating fruit, leaves or even soil that contains active chemical residue.

The long-term risks to anyone who is exposed to pesticides are difficult to calculate, but cannot be ignored.

The storage and use of pesticides (including fungicides and herbicides) is controlled. In general the advice given on pesticide labels must be adhered to.

Food: a number of gardeners or horticultural projects grow fruit and vegetables for their own consumption, and choose to produce this food without the use of chemicals. Some of those growing food are interested in the possibility of getting a better price for produce grown without using pesticides.

Cost: horticulturists looking for cheaper alternatives to chemical pesticides find that many non-chemical methods of pest-control are less expensive, although they may require more labour.

Environmental issues: many people are concerned about the effects of chemical pesticides on the environment and prefer to keep their use to a minimum or to do without them altogether.

The pest/enemy balance

All pests have natural enemies – predators, parasites or disease-causing organisms. Growing crops for food or amenity purposes usually disturbs the balance of pest/enemy populations, allowing the pest population to reach a level where it causes serious damage. This situation is made worse by using pesticides that wipe out the natural enemies along with the pest. If natural enemies are encouraged, they can have a significant effect on the level of the pest population, reducing it to a point where little damage is caused.

*　　*　　*

Outdoor crops

Some examples of natural enemies

Hoverflies: Most people know that ladybirds prey on aphids, but in fact some species of hoverfly are much more efficient predators. It has been shown, for example, that a single larva of the species *Syrphus ribesii* can eat about 600 peach-potato aphids in 15 days. Other hoverfly species eat different species of aphids.

Anthocorid bugs: The *Anthocoridae* family includes some useful predators, commonly called anthocorid bugs. These are small (4 mm. long) brown and black bugs that eat a range of pests including aphids, caterpillars and mites.

Lacewings: There are a number of different species in each of the three families of lacewings – green, brown and powdery. Between them, they prey on a range of pests, including mites and aphids.

It is a good policy, where possible, to avoid killing these, or any of the many other beneficial insects. However, natural enemies alone will not usually be enough to control pests on outdoor crops because many factors, such as weather changes, can affect the pest/enemy balance in favour of the pest. The good news is that there are a number of non-chemical methods of pest-control, in addition to several chemical methods that are approved for use on organically-grown crops.

Non-chemical methods

Through experience and research, organic growers have found many non-chemical means to prevent and control both pests and diseases. This summary provides an introduction:

- Improve the condition of the soil. Add plenty of compost to boost the humus content. This is a basic step towards growing healthier plants and reducing the risk of disease. Good drainage is also important.
- Avoid introducing pests. If you buy or swap plant material, check that it is clear of pests.
- Rotate crops. Many diseases and pests, such as eelworm, can be prevented by using suitable rotation.
- Hygiene. Pests and diseases can be harboured in rotting leaves, stumps, etc. Keep the growing area free of rubbish, and dispose of plant material, either by composting it or, if it contains pests that will not be killed by composting, by burning.
- Know your pests. In the life cycle of each pest, there are usually some weak points. Some common garden techniques exploit these. For example, pinching out the tips of broad beans in late May or early June removes early colonies of blackfly. Spraying can also be timed to coincide with the pest's most vulnerable stages. For instance, the larvae of the pea moth have to move from the stems and outsides of the pods where they hatch, into the pods. Spraying about a week after the first flowering will catch most of the caterpillars before they enter the pods.
- Barriers and traps. The type of barrier or trap to use depends on the behaviour of the pest. Carrot root fly, for example, is attracted by the scent of carrot thinnings and, once close to the crop, sights the foliage and flies in low to the ground. A clear polythene barrier (about 0.5 cm. high) supported by posts and placed around the carrot bed will screen the foliage from most of the flies.
- **Slugs:** Metaldehyde, contained in slug pellets, is poisonous to all animals and birds. There are many ways of trapping slugs – using milk or beer and water in bottles or dishes sunk into the ground, or floppy cabbage leaves spread with beef dripping, to name a few! But you do need to trap a lot of slugs to make any difference to crop damage. On a small scale it may be better to protect seedlings using cardboard milk cartons (top and bottom removed, placed over seedling and pushed into the ground). The slugs will go on eating the wax coating for some time – hopefully until the seedling has grown enough to survive. A solution of alum kills slugs on contact, and is harmless to birds and mammals.

Chemicals approved for organic pest-control

Traditional organic means of pest-control are listed below. The chemicals listed below kill insect pests but spare many beneficial insects. In addition, they break down quickly and do not accumulate in food chains. Some, however, are poisonous to people and should be used with care.

- **DERRIS** – liquid or dust. *Kills aphids, caterpillars, some weevils, flea beetle.* **Spares bees, hoverflies.** Harmless to mammals; harmful to fish, toads, ladybirds.

- **QUASSIA** – solution with soap. *Kills aphids, small caterpillars, some mites.* **Spares bees, hoverflies, ladybirds, anthocorid bugs.**

- **ELDER SPRAY** – solution of elder wood with soap. *Kills aphids, small caterpillars* (also fungicide). **Spares bees, ladybirds, anthocorid bugs.** Kills hoverflies.

- **SOFT SOAP** – soap/detergent solution. Green soft soap best. *Kills aphids, small caterpillars.* **Spares bees, ladybirds, hoverflies, lacewing, anthocorid bugs.**

Other insecticides include pyrethrum, ryania and a range of herbal and homeopathic preparations.

Approved fungicides include formaldehyde, lime sulphur, dispersable sulphur and copper fungicide.

NO herbicides or growth inhibitors are cleared.

Protected crops

Several features of protected cropping encourage the build-up of pests and diseases to damaging proportions:

- Enclosing a crop under polythene or glass enables the grower to manipulate the environment to provide optimum conditions for plant growth. This artificial environment can also provide ideal conditions for pests and disease, which can be more prolific on a given crop when it is grown under protection.
- The same crop is often grown year after year, allowing pests in the soil or on the greenhouse structure to become established.
- Protected crops have a high value, so pesticides are used intensively, with the result that pests develop resistance. Commercial growers of tomatoes, cucumbers and chrysanthemums are all experiencing this problem. Treatments developed to tackle resistance are even more costly.

Using natural enemies

The use of natural enemies is now commonplace in those areas of the glasshouse industry that experience the worst problems with pesticide resistance, and there are a number of commercial firms involved in research and development of natural enemies and in selling these and related products. Some firms now produce information and handy packs of biological control products, designed for small-scale use.

Natural enemies of greenhouse pests

Phytoseiulus persimilis is a predatory mite which is widely used to control greenhouse *red spider mite*. It is easily used by amateurs and

comes supplied on leaves or in an applicator. **Encarsia formosa** is a small wasp which lays its eggs in the larvae of *whitefly* – common pest of tomatoes and other greenhouse plants. You can obtain *Encarsia* on pieces of card. Hang these in your glasshouse, according to instructions, as soon as you see the first adult whiteflies. The parasitic wasp is effective at temperatures of 12°–15°C (54–59°F). Also available: **Cryptolaemus montrouzieri** – a ladybird which preys on *mealy bugs*. This is used on permanent collections of greenhouse ornamentals. **Amblyseius cucumeris** – a mite which preys on *thrips*, especially those attacking peppers. **Dacnusa siberica** and **Diglyphus isea** – are both insects that parasitize *leaf-miner* in chrysanthemum and tomato crops.

Pesticides and natural enemies

Ask the supplier of natural enemies which pesticides will not be harmful to these insects, as it may be necessary to use pesticides as well, if the parasite is not giving full control. Check your crop regularly for signs of pest build-up. If instructions for introducing the enemy are adhered to, you should get effective pest-control.

If you are avoiding conventional chemical pesticides, soft soap or derris kill the adult whitefly, leaving the wasp parasite and whitefly larvae unharmed. Spray every five days until the parasite has regained control.

A product called 'Savona' is available which is based on a mixture of organic fatty acids. It kills *adult whitefly* on contact – you spray the tops of the plants where adults congregate. Savona is 100% biologically degradable and no residue is left once it dries.

Biological pesticides

These are used in much the same way as chemical pesticides. However, they are based on disease-causing organisms that affect certain pests:

Bacillus thuringiensis. The spores and crystals of this bacterium are lethal to most butterfly and moth caterpillars, but harmless to everything else. Products that contain *Bacillus thuringiensis* are applied just as you would conventional sprays. The caterpillars die within one to five days of eating the bacterium; uneaten spores are destroyed by sunlight. There is no accumulation in the food-chain; if birds, for example, eat the dead caterpillars they are not harmed. *Bacillus thuringiensis* can be used on protected crops, against *tomato moth*, for example, and on outdoor crops wherever caterpillars are a pest. It is very useful against *cabbage white caterpillar*, but ensure that both surfaces of the leaves are sprayed.

Verticillium lecanii. There are two strains of this fungus which are specific biological pesticides for different pests. One strain, sold as Mycotal, kills *whiteflies* in greenhouses; the other, sold as Vertalec, is mainly used against *aphids* on greenhouse chrysanthemums.

Prevention is better than cure

- Hygiene. It is very important to clean all the fittings and structure of your greenhouse, paying particular attention to crevices where pests can overwinter. During the growing season, remove rubbish regularly. If you have trouble with soil-borne pests, soil should be sterilized, or use growbags which contain sterile compost.
- Check your greenhouse crop regularly for signs of pests. A small hand lens can be a useful aid. Get to know what pests to expect, so that you can be ready to take appropriate action when they appear.
- Check plants that you buy or swap for signs of pests.
- Weeds outside the greenhouse can provide a good jumping-off point for pests, so keep the area free of weeds.

House plants can be afflicted by a number of pests including red spider mite, aphids or whitefly. You can use the safe insecticides listed earlier, or natural enemies, *Phytoseiulis* or *Encarsia*. The best small-scale remedy for removing red spider mite on houseplants is to dab at the mites with a piece of Blu-tack rolled into a pointed shape.

Biological Control/Biological Pesticides and Suppliers

Pest	Control	Product	Suppliers (in UK)
Whitefly (glasshouse cucumbers tomatoes, peppers, ornamentals)	*Verticillium lecanii* (fungus strain)	Mycotal	Microbial Resources Fargo Bunting & Sons Natural Pest Control
Whitefly (as above)	*Encarsia formosa* (wasp – parasitic)	*Encarsia* En-strip (*Encarsia* on paper strips)	Bunting & Sons Natural Pest Control Applied Horticulture English Woodlands Koppert (UK) Fargo
Red spider mite (as whitefly plus strawberry/ ornamentals under polythene)	*Phytoseiulus persimilis* (mite – predator)	*Phytoseiulus* Spidex (*Phytoseiulus* in applicator)	Bunting & Sons Natural Pest Control English Woodlands Applied Horticulture Koppert (UK) Fargo
Aphids (glasshouse chrysanthemums)	*Verticillium lecanii* (fungus strain)	Vertalec	Microbial Resources Fargo Bunting & Sons Natural Pest Control
Lepidopterous larvae e.g., tomato moth	*Bacillus thuringiensis* (bacteria)	Biobit Bactospeine Dipel	Microbial Resources Koppert (UK) English Woodlands
Mealy bug (permanent plant collections/ glasshouse ornamentals)	*Cryptolaemus montrouzieri* (ladybird – predator)	*Cryptolaemus*	Bunting & Sons Natural Pest Control English Woodlands
Thrips (peppers)	*Amblyseius cucumeris* (mite – predator)	*Amblyseius*	Koppert (UK) Fargo
Leaf miner (chrysanthemum/tomato)	*Dacnusa siberica* (insect – parasite) *Diglyphus isea* (insect – parasite)	*Dacnusa* *Diglyphus* both parasites	Bunting & Sons English Woodlands English Woodlands Koppert (UK) Fargo

TWENTY THREE

My garden

From small beginnings gardens grow, step by step with all the successes and failures. No matter where you start, or what resources you have, the important thing is to begin, to sow that seed, take that cutting, plant that tree, ask for help. All gardeners go down this path and here are some extracts of stories from some gardeners.

Tucked away behind a busy city shopping centre is a tiny cottage garden crowded with colourfully planted tubs and raised beds. The gardener, Ann – now in her eighties – tends her three-by-five metre patch in a style of all her own, reflecting her delight in flowers, garden lore and wildlife.

'Most of the things you saw when you came before are growing. I just changed over from the spring. I had daffodils, narcissi, tulips. I buy most of my bulbs from Wards up in Northgate Street. I get my little plants – Busy Lizzies – from the market and I grew the carnations from cuttings myself. They were out there all the winter, they stood out underneath that window and they rooted. I have still got a little bit of honeysuckle out; as soon as you get a bit of cold weather the birds go for the berries. That's the birds' hideout there; they get in in the morning and they wait

for me to feed them. All sorts . . . sparrows, starlings, blackbirds, thrushes. I get water wagtails as well, from the river, and the blue tits and the green tits – they always come to empty the nuts.

'The sweet peas I grew from seed. These yellow daisies always grow like a weed. There's stocks in there, Busy Lizzies, carnations, asters and chrysanthemums in that round bed. Those are grapes. When it's cold and dry the birds come down for water and moisture so I put out the grapes that have gone off, and they will pick them all off and leave me the stems. They'll leave me the cherry stones and cherry stems, and if I cut an apple in half they'll eat all the apple inside and leave me the skin to pick up. It is unbelievable when you come to see it.

'I can't say I have got a favourite flower. They are all flowers to me and I think as much of one as I do another. I have always been like that. Right from a child I used to go out flowering and I used to pick all sorts of wild flowers. I lived in Wiltshire – Corsham and Lacock way. You could pick them in those days; we used to bring home violets, primroses, anemones and celandines and put them in vases. At Easter time when we were children we used to go out on the Good Friday with a big clothes basket lined with moss, which we filled with bunches of primroses to decorate the churches.

'I can't grow any vegetables now as there's not enough space for them with the flowers, and it wouldn't pay to grow them here. I have got thyme over there and I have had some parsley, but I don't go in for a lot of herbs. No, it's flowers here for me. These are all the old fashioned flowers. I like those nicotines. The trouble is today they all want to plant in a regimental way. They want to put squares or something like they do in the parks. I put a bit in here, a bit in there and hope for the best. I just put it in and say "Grow if you want to or if you don't, then do the other thing." It nearly always grows.

'I like some scents. I can't stand lilac scent indoors as it is too strong. I like to smell the white nicotines at night but I don't like a lot of overpowering flowers, such as lilies and carnations although I like to see them outside.

'I never use sprays. I think too many sprays are used. In older days we used to save the cigarette ends and any tobacco dust and we used to put it in water and spray the roses with that. It worked just as well. A lot of sprays are killing off the bees, you see, and you want the bees to pollinate the flowers. I don't know why they are using all these sprays, I am sure. What is it? It is money, isn't it, all the time. I had a little bit of fertilizer given me but most of it on that garden is horse manure. I swear by the old-fashioned stuff.

'A lot of people come along here and look at the garden because it is unusual. I don't regiment anything. I just put things in as I think, put it in here, stick it in there. I like to see plants growing naturally. That's what I call a cottage garden. If I see anything I like I bring it home and plant it. I don't have fixed plans. That seeded itself – the white alyssum – it was round those tubs. That campanula seeded itself. I planted the seeds of the stocks and brought them on in a box, and so with the sweet peas, then I left them outside.

'I like gardening and I can content myself with it. Now if you get anybody who does gardening and likes it – not people that don't like it, and do it just for the sake of doing it – but if they like it they can lose themselves for hours and hours in a garden. They might not *do* a lot but they can lose themselves! When I feel I want a bit of fresh air, I come out and pull up a few weeds. I spend more time out here when I change the garden. I don't think I could ever live without flowers; if I didn't have a garden I would have to go and buy flowers.

'I don't bother about insects. I just let them go on. If they eat one of my primroses I let them eat it, I shan't touch it. The greenfly is everywhere,

isn't it? I don't bother with it – I don't mind a few holes. The birds come here such a lot, they pick up the slugs. They come down here and pick all the flies off the roses; you can watch them picking them off. They do the work – I don't.'

A casual chat about gardening led two friends, Bill and John – both sufferers from multiple sclerosis – to transform a garden from an inaccessible desert to a warm, inviting beauty spot.

They saw no reason why they could not continue to enjoy gardening if the design was altered – so the pair of them sat down and drew out a design for a paved garden with gently sloping access to all parts and raised planters. With the help of their families they set to it.

Bill: 'When I became ill, I thought I'd have to forget all about gardening. I used to just sit and listen to talking books because my eyesight is poor. So when John started talking about changing the garden, I was very interested.'

John: 'When we started we called ourselves the "stick and string brigade". We didn't have any proper squares or surveying tools – just did it all by eye – and used a small spirit level. Our families helped by stripping off the turf, carting it to the back of the garden... We reckoned we moved about three or four tons of top soil, as it all seemed to fit so nicely into the four planters and centre bed. It's amazing where it all went really.

'We were doing this work just bit by bit, very gradually, probably only four to six hours a week and some weeks not at all because of the weather being so bad. In fact, we built a small wall one week and had to take it down the next because the frost had got at it. Because we did the construction so gradually, we were able to adapt the design as the work progressed. For instance, the middle bed looked too big, so we bricked it in a bit. It was very interesting that even the non-dedicated gardeners in the family began to get really involved and got a tremendous amount of enjoyment out of it.

'It's lovely to have something to fiddle with as you're sitting out here. Deadheading is very relaxing. Bill has never spent so much time in the garden, everyone is pulling his leg about the suntan he's got! Its amazing what you can see as you sit here, all different types of birds, bees, hoverflies, wasps.... Look at that bee, all his pollen sacs are full up. There's an old cabbage white ... it just opens life up again for you, just sitting out here quietly raises your spirits.

'People come by and strike up conversations – not just about the garden. It starts up friendships and broadens your whole outlook. Even the neighbours have started tidying up their gardens and got interested in gardening; the able-bodied people around are encouraged as they see what can be achieved by our struggles – it has lifted peoples' standards.

'The garden has really changed life for me... we're having a barbecue on Saturday; it's a lovely peaceful place. We're going to get some climbers for the fence, clematis or honeysuckle. The bees like these Antirrhinums; it's good to know that most of the hard work is over.'

John: 'Where there's a will, there's a way. It does take effort, but it changes your attitude because you realize that not everything is impossible. It has given Bill back the freedom of his garden, opened up life again for him.'

Evelyn has advanced angina, so her gardening activities are limited. Not so her imagination – her garden is tiny, but its interest is limitless.

'Recently I have gained a lot of pleasure from an unexpected source. It came about by accident. Double-glazing was being installed in my home, and the row of small pot plants on my windowsill had to be moved for a day or two. Looking for a spare tray to put them on, I found one which I had forgotten. Years ago, when there was a craze for decorating bottles, boxes and trays with coloured mosaics, I had covered this tray with little variegated green and white tiles, making it attractive but too heavy for everyday use. It was rectangular and measured about fifteen by nine inches. I cleaned it, and began to put my small plants on it haphazardly, round one side, along the back and down the other side.

'Suddenly it began to look like a small patio, with its tiled floor surrounded by little 'trees' or 'shrubs'. There were eight plants, in their three-or-so-inch pots, and they were a random mixture, their height ranging from four to nine inches from the pot's rim. There was a small *Coleus*, a tall barrel-cactus, a winter cherry, a fat-leaved succulent, two ivies, a young Busy Lizzie, valiantly flowering, and a squat star-succulent. All that was needed was someone to walk in this little sheltered garden. I remembered I had a white plaster model, about six inches high, of a Roman woman holding a small child by her side. I found her and placed her as if she had just entered her garden. A further search through forgotten ornaments revealed a small plastic, ivory-coloured cherub on a plinth, playing pan-pipes – a souvenir of an Italian holiday. He was soon standing in front of the tall cactus, half-framed by nearby ivy leaves. The scene was completed by a miniature pottery vase, placed on the tiles in a corner. The Romans, it is said, were rather fond of urns.

'The double-glazing has been installed for some time now but I would not think of dismantling my little patio. It sits on a small table near the window, and meets the eye like a picture, but it is better than a picture, because so much of it is alive. I happened to have the tiles and the Roman figure, but now, when I look at it, other possibilities come to mind.

'Any small statuette or china figure, pale enough to stand out against the dark leaves and pots, and hardy enough to withstand sunlight or drops from the water-can, could set another scene, with one or two related items. A Japanese 'ivory' figure perhaps, with a bamboo table-mat to cover any tin or plastic tray, and a tiny china Pekinese dog, or vase; or a Dutch figure with a pair of minute clogs from holiday mementoes, on a ground of small Dutch-style bathroom wall tiles...

'Why should flowers get all the arranging? Little pot plants need not stand in stiff rows, or huddle together in pointless groups. They too, can be used in imaginative ways, which are fun to carry out. I am sure anyone could find an interesting way of displaying them.'

Ernest's pond rockery.

Ernest lost his sight as a teenager but retained his boyhood interest in gardening. His garden today reflects his passion for colour, detail, for changes in level and variety of texture.

'I see the garden in my mind's eye and it's *my* garden when I'm alone in it. I like to enjoy the form of it, and the flowers; the roses...the beautiful formation of some of the roses with partly open buds...marvellous isn't it?

'The feel of the different leaves and whether the leaves are healthy or not; whether the plant is healthy. There's a lot of difference in a healthy plant and a not-so-healthy one. I'm in a different world of my own when I'm alone in the garden, but I make it with the idea of giving pleasure to others. Not because I want to show off, or want people to think I'm a clever chap, but because the enjoyment of others enhances my own pleasure when I'm alone. I get a double benefit from it. When someone says isn't that a beauutiful red or blue and the flower is described, it just enhances what I feel and gives me a wider vision ...'

Finally a few words from Doris. Confined to a wheelchair for nearly eighty years since contracting polio as a child, she can now manage her garden which has been specially adapted. She says:

'Each day now has a wonderful beginning, because first thing each morning I wheel myself around the garden to water the flowers and herbs, which are already a picture of colour and scent. Oh how I wish that there was a thermometer which could register my joy – it would rise to a great height!'

Appendices

About Horticultural Therapy

The Society for Horticultural Therapy (HT) is the UK national charity set up in 1978 to provide advice, information and support to elderly and disabled gardeners and those who work with them.

HT helps by:

- **Training** – Occupational Therapists and others using horticulture in their work with people with all kinds of disadvantages, so that they feel confident in their skills to lead others in gardening activities and to develop successful therapy programmes.
- **Project Advice** – for those about to set up horticultural projects to benefit people in care settings – so that they can be sure of the best chance of horticultural and therapeutic success.
- **Land Use Volunteer Service** – which enables skilled young horticulturists to use their energy and expertise to get projects started and learn about working with people at the same time.
- **Growth Point** – the magazine which keeps people and projects in touch with new developments, interesting ideas and solutions to common problems and which tries to relieve the isolation felt by many carers and clients.
- **Demonstration Gardens** – local bases for groups and individuals to get encouragement in gardening, try out facilities and see ideas in action.
- **Advice and Workshop Service** – answering thousands of queries a year from individuals with simple or serious problems with their gardening; offering practical demonstrations around the country.
- **Advisory Committee for Blind Gardeners** – answers questions and organizes practical weekends and seminars for visually impaired gardeners and those who work with them.

Membership of HT means that you:

- receive **Growth Point**, HT's quarterly magazine, free
- get help with your gardening problems
- hear from others, and swap ideas, plants, recipes, seeds
- buy tools, aids, sundries and publications at a reduced cost
- hear about workshops and study days first
- use HT's library and information services
- advertise free in **Growth Point**
- meet others at HT's Annual Meeting
- help other gardeners with special needs

Find out more from
Horticultural Therapy, Goulds Ground, Vallis Way, Frome, Somerset BA11 3DW or ring Frome (0373) 64782

Useful publications on gardening for disabled and disadvantaged people

1. Available from HT

HT 'BOOKSHOP'
A catalogue of over 80 information leaflets on a range of topics for disabled and handicapped gardeners and those who work with them. Available free on request.

GROWTH POINT
The quarterly magazine for gardeners with special needs and those who work with them. Free to members of HT, also by subscription or by single issues.

LIBRARY FACILITIES
HT has a unique collection of published and unpublished material relating to horticulture and gardening for disabled and disadvantaged people. Details of the facilities and its uses are contained in the HT 'BOOKSHOP'.

GARDENING IS FOR EVERYONE
Audrey Cloet and Chris Underhill
Souvenir Press 1982
£4.95 paperback. Also available from book-shops.

A practical handbook of weekly indoor and outdoor gardening activities through the year. Particularly suitable for people with handicaps, gardening clubs and those planning activities for groups.

2. Available from the Federation to Promote Horticulture for Disabled People

A selection of publications on therapeutic horti-culture.
Details available from John Catlin, 242 The Ridgeway, Enfield Middx. EN2 8AP.

3. Other publications

CITY FARMER

The quarterly magazine for Community Gardens and City Farms. Published by the National Federation of City Farms Ltd, The Old Vicarage, 66 Fraser Street, Windmill Hill, Bedminster, Bristol BS3 4LY. Tel. 0272 660663.

Individual copies 75p. Yearly subscription £4. Contains news, views, ideas, advice and information on City Farms and Community Gardens. Also lists all member gardens and farms.

CITY FARMING AND COMMUNITY GARDENING

Christopher Wardle. Ed. Kay Knights 1983. Inter Change Books.

£3.95 from bookshops or from Inter Change, 15 Wilkins St, London NW5 3NG. Tel. 071-267 9421.

Comprehensive information on how to set up and run a neighbourhood City Farm and Community Garden in Britain.

GARDENING AND THE HANDICAPPED CHILD

Patricia Elliot. Disabled Living Foundation 1978.

£4.10 inc p & p. Available from Haigh & Hochland, The Precinct Centre, Oxford Rd, Manchester M13 9QA. Tel. 061-273 4156.

Inspiration for teachers and instructors – full of ideas. Practical and educational aspects, hobbies, further education, employment. Useful appendices – bibliography, addresses, suppliers.

GARDENING IN RETIREMENT

Alec Bristow. RHS Wisley Handbook.

£3.95 plus £1 p & p from RHS Enterprises, Wisley Gardens, Wisley, Woking, Surrey GU23 6QB. Tel. 0483-211113.

An overview of gardening in later years.
Contains many ideas and practical tips on design, etc.

GARDENING IN RETIREMENT

Isobel Pays. Age Concern.

£1.95 from bookshops or from Age Concern, 60 Pitcairn Road, Mitcham, Surrey CR4 3LL. Tel. 081-640 5432.

Contains ideas for adapting an existing garden for more efficient maintenance and for increased enjoyment as you have more time to spend. Foreword by Dame Vera Lynn and an introduction by Percy Thrower.

GARDENING WITHOUT SIGHT

Kathleen Fleet. RNIB.

£2.50 inc. p & p from RNIB, 224 Portland Street, London W1N 6AA. Tel. 071-388 1266.

Invaluable and very practical guide for gardeners with visual impairments.

Gardening books in Braille are available on loan from:
- National Library for the Blind, Cromwell Road, Branbury, Stockport, Cheshire.

COME GARDENING and the CASSETTE LIBRARY FOR BLIND GARDENERS

Annual subscription £2.

Miss Kathleen Fleet, 48 Tolcarne Drive, Pinner, Middx HA5 2DQ.

Come Gardening (formerly *The Gardener*) is a quarterly magazine for visually impaired gardeners. Produced on cassette tape and in braille it comprises articles, news, ideas, gardening queries and product information. Subscription also covers the Cassette Library with its wide range of gardening subjects.

KEEP ON GROWING

Susan Hale. Herefordshire DIAL 1985.

£1.25 inc p & p. Available from Herefordshire DIAL, 15 St Owen St., Hereford HR1 2JB. Tel. 0432 277 770

A Herefordshire guide for disabled and elderly gardeners. Tips and techniques, local nurseries, garden centres, stockists and gardens to visit in Hereford and Worcester.

GARDENING

Compiled by D Hollinrake. Eds G M Cochrane & E R Wilshere.

1st edition 1987. Equipment for the Disabled. £6.00 inc. p & p from Equipment for the Disabled (Dept EU), Mary Marlborough Lodge, Nuffield Orthopaedic Centre, Headington, Oxford OX3 7LD. Tel. 0865 750103.

Invaluable and comprehensive information on garden design, plants, tools, safety, propagation, resources, bibliography, clubs for disabled gardeners, etc.

OUT OF DOORS WITH HANDICAPPED PEOPLE

Mike Cotton. Human Horizons Series, Souvenir Press 1981. £4.50 from bookshops.

Intended for use by handicapped young people themselves, by their parents and teachers. An illustrated guide to the environment of towns, parks and gardens, woodlands, farms, seashore and moors and mountains. Contains many practical ideas for activities.

THERAPEUTIC HORTICULTURE

Rosemary Hagedorn. Winslow Press 1987. £12.95 from bookshops.

Aimed primarily at Occupational Therapists, contains lots of useful information on special designs, therapeutic analysis, task content, programming, safety, techniques, etc.

Also includes an invaluable list of references and sources of information.

4. Tools and equipment

Information on tools, sundries and equipment is constantly changing. For up-to-the-minute information on manufacturers, suppliers and prices, contact Horticultural Therapy.

Useful organizations

United Kingdom
GARDENING FOR DISABLED TRUST
 Church Cottage, Headcorn, Kent TN27 9NP.
 Practical help with gardening for disabled
 people, including grants to individuals.

United States of America
AMERICAN HORTICULTURAL THERAPY
ASSOCIATION
 9220 Wightman Road, Suite 300, Gaithers-
 burgh, Maryland 20879. Tel. 301 948 3010.
 The American Horticultural Therapy Association (AHTA) is the professional association
 for horticultural therapists in the USA. It
 recognizes and registers horticultural therapists through a voluntary professional regis-
 tration programme. It also offers a range of
 services.
 Because it has a wide spread of members, it
 has contacts with many organizations throughout the USA.
 Many Botanic Gardens in the USA run
 horticultural therapy programmes. For details
 of what goes on in your area, contact your
 nearest Botanic Gardens.

Canada
CANADIAN HORTICULTURAL THERAPY
ASSOCIATION
 c/o Royal Botanic Gardens, P.O. Box 399,
 Hamilton, Ontario L8N 3H8.
 The Canadian Horticultural Therapy Association exists to provide education and guidance
 in programme development to persons using
 horticulture as therapy in community agencies
 and institutions, to secure recognition of horticulture as an effective therapy, and to establish and maintain contact with similar
 organizations.
 As in the United States, many Botanic
 Gardens run their own horticultural therapy
 programmes.

Index